Mom No More

Coping with the Late-Life Loss of

Adult Children

One Woman's Story

Large
Print

Mom
no more

*Coping with the Late-Life Loss of Adult Children -
One Woman's Story*

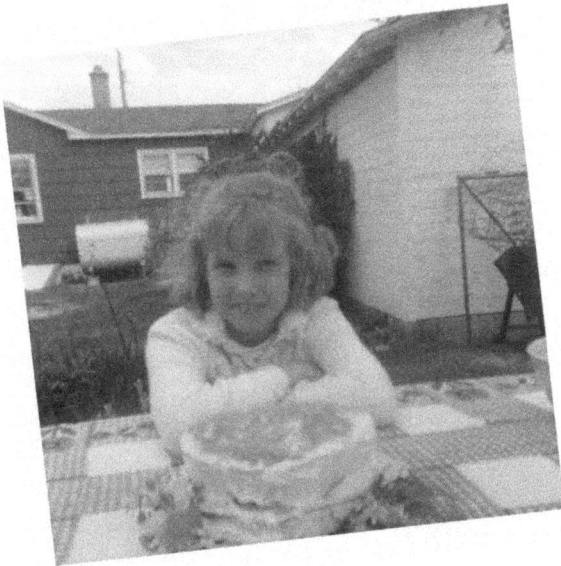

Hatala Geroproducts • Greentop, Missouri

Published in the United States of America
by Hatala Geroproducts, Greentop, MO 63546

(pop 427)
09 08 07 06 05 1 2 3 4 5

Mom No More: Coping with the Late-Life Loss of Adult
Children -   One Woman's Story
by M. Mignon Matthews

ISBN-13: 978-1-933167-32-9

LCCN: 2008927134

Cover Design: Bryan De Guzman
Cover and interior photos: M. Mignon Matthews
Composition: Age Positive Editorial Services

DEDICATED TO THE LOVES OF MY LIFE

This is dedicated to the memory of Eva Lois and Albert Louis Gunzenhauser, my son and daughter, who brought such sunshine into my life and left me much too soon. Eva died on February 7, 1980, at the age of 18 and Albert died on January 28, 2005, at the age of 41.

Eva (Evie) died three months before she would have graduated from High School. She was so proud of being a senior and so excited about the approaching graduation. She was talented in many ways. Eva played guitar and sang, she wrote beautiful verse and she was showing promise with her paintings. Some of her poetry has been included in this book. Eva did not live to marry or have children, she did not have time to go to college or start a career, but she touched many lives and, most of all, those of her family.

Albert, too, was musically talented and artistically gifted, but he did not take much time to develop those talents or his gift with the written word. He married, raised a family and worked hard in construction to give them the things that they needed and wanted. He rose from Apprentice to Journeyman and from there to the position of Superintendent. He was good at the job and at managing the men who worked for him. He earned their respect and, in many cases, their friendship. He cared about what he did, but what he cared about most were his children. He was an outstanding father, a loving husband, a devoted son and a steadfast friend.

I miss both of them every day.

Table of Contents

Foreword

No Title for Us   13
   The Club   15
Learning to Be Alone   17
Expectations   21
   Broken Wings   27
The Early Years   29
We Move   33
   Summer Days   38
Life Lessons   41
   A Cat   49
Our Family Ends   51
   The Rose   57
All About Me   59
   This Too Shall Pass   65
Shadows on My Heart   67
   Baby Brother   71
Dark Days   73
   Mom   80
Imagine If You Dare   81
   Lost in Memory   85
Chill Wind   87
   Borrowed Blessings   94
Messages from Evie   97
   Driven   99
Patti O'Kat   101
   Fur Persons   105

Hallmark & Rockwell   107
    Christmas   112
Imagine My Surprise   113
    Furniture   116
Why?   117
    The Voice Inside   128
Grief   129
    Debut   137
    My Favorite Room   138
The Dream   139
    About Dreams   143
Two Years   145
    In Season   149
Staying Connected   151
All About Family   157
    Two Years   163
Looking Back   165
    Two Plus Twenty-Five   172
Grandchildren   175
    Umbrellas   178
All About My Health   179
Two Forward, One Back   185
Denouement   191
    Write-On   193

Foreword

I approached this book with great interest; it relates to research I've conducted on childlessness, suffering, and forgiveness. What I found in my research and in this book, is that the small, personal story of a "little life," when told with honesty and insight, becomes a metaphor for everyone's journey through life.

The major experiences in Mignon's story are the losses of her children, her daughter at age 18; her son at age 41. The tragedy of losing two children seems too much for anyone to bear. Although Mignon recognizes that her grief is never ending, she acknowledges that she has been placed in a position, in the latter stages of life, to make choices about accepting the mystery of death, continuing to ask the why of suffering or simply live the question, and creating a reason to live when the ostensible reasons to go on—one's children—are gone.

Mignon knows how to tell a story; all necessary elements are present: childhood loneliness foreshadows unexpected loneliness in later life; the recounting of her children's tragic deaths; the search, after the children are gone and jobs have fallen through, to re-discover life's purpose. She brings authentic emotions to life, such as gratitude for dreams about marriage and motherhood that came true, the happiness she found as a wife and mother, if only for a little while, and the sweet comfort of beloved pets. She also exposes the range of feelings that occur after profound loss, such as the terrible fear that often attends grief, a hint of joy emerging on a winter morning that suddenly turns (because of a scent or a song) into renewed sorrow.

There are perhaps not many of us who will face what Mignon faced. Yet, we can identify with her story because we are more like her than not. For many people, the latter stages of life become a time of mourning. We lose loved ones, good health, worldly goods, and relationships. Through these losses, we suffer, question, try to find meaning, and decide either to move on or give up.

Mignon shows us that life may take away what we thought was our central role in life, such as being a mother, a wife, or a hard worker. And even after this role is gone, life may take something more, such as our illusion that if we are kind to others and work hard, we will succeed in love and work. We may be asked, like Mignon was asked at points in her life, to simply "be," and to rest in our lack of control over the ultimate issues we face as human beings: life and death. We may be shown that our central role was not about "me" at all, but about remaining a fellow-traveler on this journey when we would prefer to stop or get off.

This is a good book, a very good book.

Helen K. Black, PhD
Center for Applied Research on Aging and Health
Thomas Jefferson University

Preface

(Note from the Author)

My life has had its moments; it has been fun, exciting, painful and ordinary in turn, which would describe the lives of most of the people on this planet. Those of us who survive those painful events have learned to cope in some way. One of my coping mechanisms has been reading. The other most significant coping mechanism for me was writing in my journals.

When my son Albert died, I was 66 years old and two years into retirement. It felt like a lethal blow, but I had learned when I lost my daughter Eva, that one makes a decision to live or to die when such tragedies strike. Because I believe that everyone and everything happens for a reason and because I was still living, I chose life again.

Once more, I tried to find my way, and that path led to this book. If you are reading it, it is likely that you too have suffered a heartbreaking loss of some kind.

I hope my story helps.

No Title for Us

A widow is a woman whose husband has died and a widower is a man whose wife has died. An orphan is a child whose parents are both dead, but what is a woman or a man whose children are dead? There isn't any title for us; yet, we exist. It would help to know how others like me cope, but I don't know one man or woman personally who has lost their entire family and that makes me feel even more alone. There is comfort in sharing with someone who walks in your shoes.

As I write this, it is the year 2006 and I am 67 years old; my "family" consists of two dearly loved cats. I have so much maternal instinct left and only the cats on whom to squander it. I gladly apply it to my grandchildren when I see them, but that is a very rare occasion indeed. They are teenagers and busy with their own lives; also, I suspect that it may make them sad to see me. They know how much I loved their father and how alone I am without him.

My daughter died at the age of 18 in 1980 and my son at the age of 41 in 2005. My marriage was over or, as my son put it, "our family ended," before I lost my oldest child and only daughter. When I lost Evie, I still had Albert, was in a committed relationship and held down two jobs. Twenty-five years later when I lost Albert, my only son, I was retired and no longer had parents, siblings or many other relatives. I felt truly alone. He was my "rock," my connection to life, my reason to be.

I have been advised to journal, which I have done. It helped me to pour out the feelings onto paper, especially because there was no one with whom I felt that I could share all of them. Things became clearer as I wrote and when re-reading at a later date, it helped me to benchmark my progress through the maze.

This work includes selected pages from those journals, which were written at different times as I tried to take in my loss and then find a way to live the rest of my life. It also includes poetry, some of mine, written at different times in my life, and some of Evie's, written in the late 70's.

I have found books on losing a child, the unfairness of life and other related topics, but I have not found anything that spoke to my specific situation; therefore, I decided to put something together in the hope that others coping in a similar situation may relate to my ramblings and that they will feel less alone.

That said, I don't mean to imply that I have solved all the problems, beaten the pain and got a wonderful new life going; not true. What I have going is a life in progress, one that I live day by day trying to make good decisions and do the right things. Putting my personal experience in print seemed like the right thing for me to do and my hope is that others will agree.

The Club

I joined a club, but not by choice, many years ago;
A club no mother wants to join and never wants to go
To meet that band of mournful souls who lost a precious child,
A child who is missed every day, on whom misfortune smiled.

What did she know, how did she feel, what could I have done
To keep her with me, keep her safe, to keep her; and, my son?
Perhaps, misfortune did not smile or her or yet on him.
Misfortune smiled on me, it seems, and my life looks quite grim.

I only had her eighteen years, but kept him forty-one.
Forty-one years is a very short time for a mother to keep her son.
Her childhood had been left behind; her grown up life just
started.
They left too soon and left their Mom forever brokenhearted.

The Author, age 3

Learning to Be Alone

It seems to me that very few people have been as well trained to be alone as me. Mom was there in body, but often not in mind. She wasn't crazy. She was an intelligent, loving and chronically depressed woman. Sometimes she put on a happy face, which I early learned to imitate, but she was deeply sad. She would read me stories and the Bible, which I did not understand; still, I sat quietly and listened as bidden to do. I loved the stories and learned to love to read.

We lived on the side of a mountain with no children near my age within what Mother considered walking distance. I was more than willing to walk across the creek and road (there was a bridge) to play with younger children, but was rarely permitted that opportunity. Mother's reasons were: 1) the dangers in crossing the road, which had very little traffic in the 40's and, in fact, still has very little traffic. 2) that my visit would be inconvenient to the family that I so wanted to visit. Why not? I was certainly an inconvenience to mother, having arrived unexpectedly when she was 39 years of age, and my brother and sister were 15 and 13 respectively.

Consequently, I was often thrown back on my own resources. I did have toys, many handed down from my siblings, but some of my own. I still have an attachment to two dolls, Gloria Mignon and Pinkey. Gloria Mignon was a gift from my Aunt Nonnie; she wore a pretty yellow organdy dress and said MaMa. I got her as a new doll which did not often happen. Pinkey arrived in a cradle made from an oatmeal box. Mother had re-dressed her and made the cradle by covering half the oatmeal container in fabric. I thought it beautiful and, even better, Pinkey drank a bottle and wet. That was a wonderful gift for me.

I played with dolls, and with equal enthusiasm, I enjoyed paper dolls. I even photographed them when I got my first camera from my brother for Christmas. I made clothing for my paper dolls out of wallpaper samples. I had tea parties with my real dolls inside and, when weather permitted, outside. I especially liked to put them in the doll carriage and push them into the woods by a little stream, where I would set up my tea things and dolls and have our tea party.

It would have really helped if I could ride a bike, and my brother had one, so I learned on that when I got big enough. But, "the roads are too steep and you might fall off," or "you might not hear a car coming and get hit;" so, I soon tired of driving it around the apple tree and gave up biking. When I was an adult, I tried again, but could not get the hang of it (so much for that old adage).

Of course, there was school and in summer there were visiting cousins, but I had not learned how to play with other children and was ostracized for the first few years at school. My cousins were much kinder, but two or three weeks a year was the most I saw of them.

That is the basis of my training, but children are resilient and I found ways to enjoy myself. Reading was primary after I learned how and I was always one of the best readers in my classes. In the summer, when I did not have access to the library, I would scour our old farmhouse attic to see what I could find and there were books up there to be found. I read them all – no less than twice.

Summers: I so wanted to go swim in the creek, but I could not go alone, as I might drown. The water was not over my head by the time I reached the age of 10, but there are still ways I could have drowned and Mother had thought of every one. Since there was rarely anybody I could swim with, I did not swim much in the summer and never got very good at it. It is very likely that I would not have gotten good at it anyway, but we'll never know.

So my free time, summer, fall, winter and spring, was mainly divided into reading and playing the piano. Mother had instruction books and played herself, so she answered my questions and I hammered away. I had to. Daddy said that he would chop up the piano for kindling wood if I did not learn to use two hands soon and I believed him.

As I entered my teens, I got involved in extra curricular activities at school and church and spent less time alone. But, the groundwork was laid and I was prepared to be a loner. This does not mean that I wanted to be alone; I was terrified that would happen to me. My mother was always convinced that her health was failing and that her heart was "weak." She shared that with everyone and I could not fail to hear about it and to fear losing her. As a young child, she was the most important person in my life and every day that I went to school, I feared that she would be dead when I got home. That never happened and she lived to be seventy years of age, but fear of abandonment is hard to overcome and it has been a ruling factor for me throughout most of my life. If I had not been so afraid to be alone, I would not have stayed so long in a very dysfunctional marriage and my children and I would have been better off.

The way my life has turned out so far, I thank God that I did have that experience of managing my solitude. Now, both of my children are permanently gone and I am alone.

I need to "start over." I hope that I have learned the necessary lessons and have the physical and spiritual strength to do something worthwhile and gratifying with the rest of my life.

I am done playing with dolls (even though I have made new outfits for Gloria Mignon and Pinkey and keep them on display). My car is in good condition and I can visit my friends or meet them at the gym, where I can swim any time I choose. One of the activities that my friends and I favor is tea parties, so now I can invite friends for tea and conversation in my own home. Reading continues to be a great source of pleasure for me and I belong to a book club where we discuss the books that we choose to read as a group; also, I have begun to play the piano again, after many years of neglect. In fact, I have volunteered to be the musician for one of the clubs I recently joined and accompany group singing for ceremonies.

It's all up to me now and there are options available. My history has laid the groundwork for me to live the life I've been dealt and, with God's help, I'll find my way.

Expectations

"Don't expect anything much and you won't be disappointed." I learned that old chestnut at a young age and I learned exactly how it worked at the same time. My parents were always poor and had lived through the Depression. There was not much to be gotten, so every thing received was treasured and saved.

As a child and young girl, I really did not like to wear "snuggies," but I always got one or two new ones for Christmas and it was good to have anything new. In case "snuggies" are unknown to the reader, they are similar to "longjohns" for women who wear skirts; knitted cotton or wool blend underwear, they reached to the knees. I welcomed their warmth, but they were so unfashionable and I could not let any of my schoolmates see them for fear of more teasing and embarrassment. They did not have to wear such things, because they had central heat in their homes; something we could not afford. It would have been a little better to get the snuggies just because I needed them and not for Christmas gifts, but I adjusted my expectations and was grateful. I usually got one new flannel nightgown for Christmas too and that was a lovely treat. I remember one that had ruffled sleeves and a big ruffle at the bottom, it was blue and the flannel was soft and I felt pretty in it, besides being warm and snug.

So, I learned what I might expect, which "must be"

what I deserved, early on and it has followed me all of my life. I so wanted a happy marriage, but did not ever really expect it and did not know what one looked like. When my husband gave me enough money to buy food and there was some money to clothe the children, I was grateful and if he was out every night; well, he eventually came home to me and I could pretend that was OK.

Sometime in the 1970's, when I did raise my marital expectations and try for more, life stamped down on me, HARD. The children started acting out and I feared for them. Their behavior was partly because they were teen-agers, but as our arguments escalated and the marital situation worsened, they began taking their rebellion to new levels. I arranged for counseling for them, which helped to an extent, but after a few sessions the therapist took me aside and said, "I can repair the hole in the roof and replace the broken windows, but if the foundation does not get some attention, the house will still fall down." So, we went for marital counseling. My husband thought it a waste of time, but since I appeared to be having a problem, he agreed to go to a few sessions. There was an argument about going to each session and, usually, more argument when we left. I decided that my best option was to go myself and learn how to better cope with the situation and that is what I did. By now, neither of the children was willing to participate either; and, taking them against their wishes was not successful.

I continued to work with the therapist, but some months later my husband moved out. He deeded the house to me and left the state. About eight months after he separation, Evie and I had a serious disagreement about a boy she was dating and I told her that she was not to see him anymore. She knew and understood my reasons, but did not agree that she should not see him and when I returned home from work one afternoon, I found her room empty. Her father had returned a few months before and she had moved in with him and his friend.

I came to a point where I knew that I could not continue living in our marital home. It was too much to maintain and my husband still behaved as though he lived there. The children were torn between us and the situation was not good. The house had been deeded to me when we initially parted, and one of my associates at the college library where I worked was looking to buy a house in the area. I sold it to him and made plans to move to a different location where I felt more secure and which I could afford and manage.

When I made my plans, I assumed that Albert would move with me, but he chose to remain in the area and live with his father and sister. Moving with me would have meant a new school, although it was not that distant that he would not see his sister, father and friends. When we sat down to discuss "our" move, he said, "Mom, it isn't that I don't love you and want to be with you, but Dad takes me hunting and fishing and stuff. What do you do with a Mom?" That was a good question. I understood what he was saying; that I taxied him to and from activities and friend's houses was something he took for granted and assumed, I think, that his father would do the same for him. Otherwise, what I did was shop with and for him, prepare meals, take care of the house, care for him when he was sick and take him to the doctor and dentist. What fun was any of that? And, he missed his sister too. I felt hurt and betrayed, but that was where he wanted to be, and I left without either of my children.

Soon the new game began; they played "musical houses." When the rules did not suit them at one house, they left and moved to the other; sometimes, one or both of them would move in with their aunt and uncle when they were angry with their father, and spend week-ends and free time with me.

Four months before she would have graduated high school, my daughter died in her sleep and she was not even at home when it happened; she was with friends.

My son lived 41 years, and I am grateful for that, but how I do miss him every day. He has been gone for less than a year and the pain is very raw. During the course of my life, I held onto the expectation that I would have him for the rest of my life. Lightening does not strike twice in the same place, does it? I could not face the possibility of losing him when I knew what it cost me to lose her; but, I face his loss now.

I sit here alone in my condo and type these words to try and release some of the pain onto the screen (or into the database or whatever). I try to find a meaning in what happened, but I don't find it. I am retired, I am divorced, my only other attempt at marriage failed and both of my children are dead. Did my changing expectations of life have some kind of mystic impact on what happened, was it all about the randomness of living or was it fate?

After my divorce, I started a career in business as a technical trainer, and later moved into customer service management. I hoped to be a Vice President some day, but never really believed that would happen and it didn't. I did make Director and have my own department, but when the company was bought out, any hope of advancement was quickly dashed; in fact, they wanted to get rid of me and install someone of their own choosing. That is just what they did and I left at the end of 2002.

I am getting old, my health is not what it was a few years ago, I have a limited income and I feel very alone. I am told that I don't look my age and, up until this year, I did not feel my age. Now, I feel ancient and tired and much of the time, I just want to go where my children went.

What is Christmas to a woman who has lost her children and, for celebratory purposes, her grandchildren? What is any other holiday? What are my goals, what do I want, how do I put it together this time?

My mood swings can be very wide in the course of one day. I was doing "up" all day and tonight I am crashing again. There are things I can do when I crash. I can drink wine and read a book. I can eat too much. I can take a walk or go to the gym if it happens during the day. I can call a friend at any time of day, but....

Part of my upbringing instilled in me the certainty that I was inconvenient to my parents and would be to others as well; therefore, I should never expect people to want to hear from me or be with me. I have learned that is not necessarily true and I am certainly old enough to take responsibility for my expectations, but I get flushed and anxious when I call people (but not when they call me). Calling on a friend when I crash might help me get through this and I have wonderful and supportive friends, but I don't believe that I have the right, nor do I want to bring them down with my pain. I don't want to be inconvenient to my friends and chance losing them when I need them so much. So, I eat too much or drink too much wine and I gain weight, which makes me feel even worse.

I guess that is all about my early conviction that I was inconvenient to my parents. If I don't believe anybody would want me around when I am sad and they really want to be there for me, I am not being fair to them or to myself. I do know that I want to be there when those I care about need support and I am hurt if I get pushed away at such a time. There is no logic in believing that they would not feel the same way, but after 67 years, how do I convince myself now? And, how do I get past this painful time in my life without turning to my friends?

Tonight I can't find any answers; only questions.

Broken Wings

"How can I fly with two broken wings?"
The little bird cried, who no longer sings.
She staggered and stumbled and fell on the ground,
Then picked herself up without making a sound.

On wobbly legs, she headed for home
With everything hurting, all sad and alone.
It seemed a long journey, but she reached her nest
And wearily settled herself in to rest.

Into the stillness a prayer she pled
And out of the stillness a gentle voice said,
"Even though now you are feeling great pain,
The hurt can be healed and you can fly again."

She pondered and wondered if she should try
To heal up her wounds or let herself die.
Then there in the dark, a gleam came to her eye,
A glimmer of hope that she might again fly.

28

Evie's second Christmas, with Santa and
her "Kissie Doll"

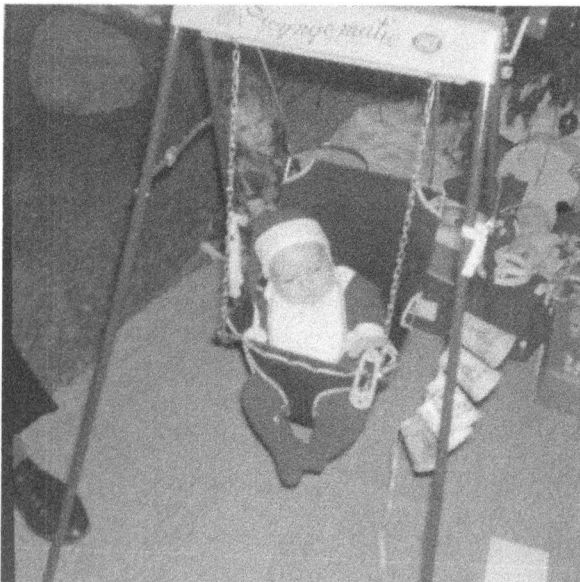

Albert's first Christmas

The Early Years

The photograph on page 64 shows Eva Lois and Albert Louis, dressed for the Christmas program at St. John's church in 1964. Her dress was dark blue velvet and his suit was lighter blue velvet. I was so proud of them and they were so excited about Santa.

That year, we were in our own house for Christmas for the first time; a two bedroom row house that we made into three bedrooms by cutting the huge bathroom in half for the baby. He was allergic to almost everything, so he had to have a dust proof room in an old house; no small challenge, but we did our best. His father built the room and I selected linoleum and paint. He could not have curtains or stuffed animals unless they were washable and he could not have carpet. We bought an air filter and I still don't know if it filtered very well, but the sound was soothing and helped him fall asleep. He never wanted to go to bed, so anything that helped was important.

How I looked forward to Christmas that year! One of our friends liked to play Santa and would get out the suit every year, so this was the second year he visited our children to take their requests. I had invited their cousins, John and David for the event and a great time was had by all.

On Christmas Eve, my husband's parents came over for eggnog and Christmas cookies and spent the evening,

enjoying the children before they went to bed (later than they should have done, of course). One of our traditions was that each child had new pajamas on Christmas Eve and this year they were candy cane striped with a little mob cap for Evie and footies for Albert. They looked so cute and I have lots of pictures. After his parents left, we got the wrapped gifts out of hiding and put them under the tree. By then, it was pretty late; but, the children were not old enough to know that THIS was the night, so we got up at the usual time and destroyed the front room before breakfast.

It was a wonderful Christmas and I remember some of the gifts we gave them. Evie got a metal stove, refrigerator and sink that could actually hold water, which could be poured out of the faucet. Albert got a rocking horse, a wagon and other age appropriate toys. I know they both got Play-Doh. What Albert did with it is what I remember most clearly, but I'm getting ahead of that story.

Their father was never a very organized person, but we could usually locate his car keys before he left the house in the morning; however, there came a time when they were nowhere to be found. Of course, I had a set and he used them while the search continued; but, he was getting quite cranky about it and the children were the chief suspects. Knowing he was careless with things, I assumed that he would find them one day exactly where he had left or dropped them and would never admit that to me; I would just find my keys returned. I was wrong. Evie found them but needed our help to recover them;

they were carefully wrapped in Play-Doh and stuffed into the reservoir of Evie's sink. The problem was that several days had elapsed (I did not let her play with water every day) and the dough had hardened into rock. Eventually, we got it and the keys out of their rock case without destroying the reservoir. Of course, the culprit was my darling baby, Albert, who had no idea that he had caused all that fuss. Once the keys were recovered, the incident became cute and his father bragged about what a clever little fellow he was to do that. All's well that ends well and that little episode ended just fine.

I still have the wooden jewelry box that Evie's father made for her that year for Christmas. He made it of pine, stained it a maple tint and put her name on the top in wooden letters that he carved out for the purpose. It is a nice box and she loved it and used it throughout her life.

That was a very good year.

Albert at Easter

Playing house in the kitchen

We Move

We had most of the improvements made to our little row house, when Al discovered a house he had to have. It was out of town with woods behind it; a real country setting. The price was right, the school was said to be better and everyone said it was a good investment. The mortgage was arranged and we moved in the spring of 1967.

I had mixed feelings about moving. Our little row house was cozy and I liked the convenience of town living. I could walk Evie to school with Albert in a stroller and could shop on the way home if I wished. We had friends in town and I felt as if I had just gotten settled. But, logic won out. There were downsides to the row house, several of them. They were old houses and I worried about the possibility of fire. Also, we had one very odd neighbor, who made me worry more about accidents, etc. I knew the row would not appreciate like the house in the country, so it was the right thing to do.

But, the country house was also a two bedroom. The living room was small and there was no dining room; just an "eat in" kitchen. There was an attached garage and shop in the back and a big back yard. My husband and I agreed that he would convert the garage into a dining/ living room after converting a small storage room with a back door into a bedroom for Albert.

Both Evie and Albert were excited and happy about

the move. They had a big yard to play in now and could chase after rabbits and toads and squirrels (oh my). In fact, one of the first things my little boy did while we were moving in was to find some toads and put them in canning jars, which he then buried in the soft dirt of the car port. Fortunately, I caught him and asked why he was doing that. He responded that he was putting them there to play with later and then I had to go into the dialog about how they would not be able to breath in the jar and they would die. He immediately began digging them up and as he had not gotten very far with his project at that point, we saved all the little toads and turned them loose to play another day.

Evie started first grade from that house and rode the school bus for the first time. She was a little anxious, but there was nothing shy about my girl and she loved it. The first complaint, actually the only complaint, I ever got from a teacher about her was when her first grade teacher asked me if I would talk to her about hugging Billy. It seems that she had developed an attachment to a little boy in her class by the name of Billy and at every opportunity she would throw both of her arms around him and hug him hard. Needless to say, Billy found this to be an embarrassing problem, but being a well behaved little boy, did not fuss about it. The teacher noticed his distress and spoke to Evie about it, but she took note that while they were lined up in the hall, Evie gave Billy another bear hug; so, she called. We talked and Billy went hugless afterward. She really did not see the problem, but would do as she was told. She was a very good little girl.

One of the photos that follow this chapter is of Albert on his first day of school and that proved to be an adventure. He went off on the bus with his sister with a huge grin on his face, so happy to be a "big kid," but at the half day when he was due home, the school bus went right on by the house. Naturally, I panicked; that is what I do in emergencies. I jumped into the car and headed down the dirt road in the direction from which the bus had come. About two miles from my house, I saw my little man stoically trudging toward home, clutching his new lunch box. He was glad to see his mom that day! It seems that he just got off the bus at the end of the road that went by our house and the bus driver allowed him to go. Guess who was on the phone to the school as soon as the PB&J was set out for my little hero? It never happened again.

They both loved school at this point in time and began making friends. Both got good grades and I only had one or two uncomfortable talks with teachers. They started out with the same statement, "We really enjoy Albert. He is such a kind, sweet boy, but he seems to think it is his mission to make everybody laugh and this disrupts the class. Please talk to him. He is a good boy, but a bit disruptive." Yes, he was loving school.

There is a photo of Evie on the cover of this book with the first Mother's Day cake that she made for me. Of course, her dad helped her, but he let her do all of the decorating and she was SO proud of all those lavender sprinkles.

Evie joined the Girl Scouts and won a prize for

selling the most cookies. She told me that it really helped that everybody at her Grandfather's wake bought so many of them. In her defense, and it sounds as if she needs one, she hardly knew her father's dad. It was his stepfather with whom she had a warm, loving relationship.

Of course, Albert had to join the Cub Scouts as soon as he was eligible and that became a major activity in our house, because his Dad agreed to be Cub Master. I am not quite sure why that made me a Den Mother, but somehow I was. And, since he went to work and I was a stay-at-home Mom, the administrative and planning parts of his job fell to me too. That said, we had a really good time with those little boys and their Den Sisters. No, there is no such designation, but Evie and her friend Mary, whose brother was also in the Den, were not to be left out of the action. They caused as much trouble for their brothers as they could get away with. We did floats for parades and "clean up the highway" projects. They sold flower bulbs to support the troops and made wishing wells with sweet potato plants in them for their mothers on Mother's Day.

This was a good time. It brought us together as a family and we had fun and made more mutual friends. The children thrived.

Albert's first day of school

Albert the Cub Scout and Evie the Sister

Summer Days

They come in dreams, they come and go
Too quickly. I wake up and know
Those days are gone and won't return;
Yet, how I wish they would and yearn
To wake to little hands and voices,
A day with only happy choices.

A messy kitchen filled with smells
Of eggs and bacon, toast and jells,
Spilled milk glides across the floor,
I wipe it up; she asks for more.
A slice of bacon moves itself
From Evie's dish to Albert's mouth.

I referee this little fuss
And send them off to get cleaned up,
Tackle the kitchen and then it's her hair;
Not her idea, there is some tangle there.
The rest of the day is more of the same;
Except, we might find time for a game.

The next day could be visiting day;
We go to see our friends and play.
My friend and I do "crafty" things
While all the children play on the swings.
We'll have some snacks; they'll jump in the pool
And then we'll go home, all wet and so cool.

Those days can't come back, but the memory lingers
And clings to my heart just like their little fingers
Would cling to my hand as they toddled first steps
And learned to cross streets and become more adept
At being grown up, independent and strong.
It happened so fast, didn't take very long.

Said goodbye to the infant, the toddler, the child;
Each stage was an ending, a loss, although mild.
I wanted to see them adult and in charge,
Living their lives and living them large.
They did while they lived, but their lives did not last.
Now, all of the joy they brought lives in the past.

Evie with a new doll and Albert as "Batman"

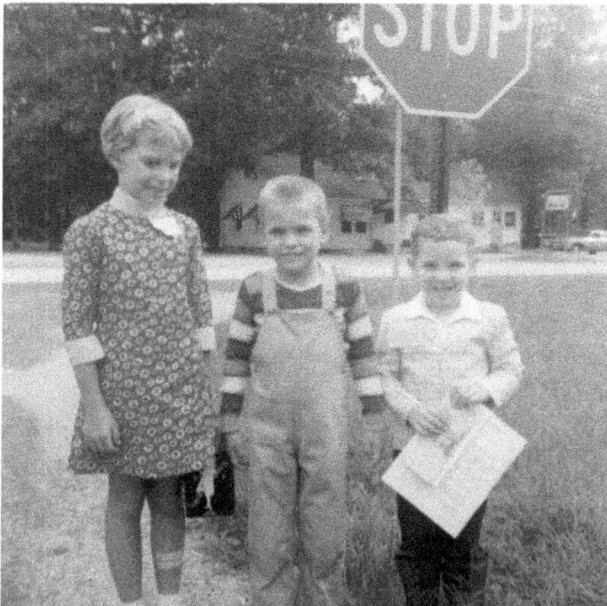

Evie, Albert, and their Cousin John

Life Lessons

If you live long enough, you accumulate losses. That is a fact and I have lived long enough to accumulate quite a few of them. My first great loss was when my grandmother died; I was 19 and I lost the one person who saw only good in me. That was 1958. My mother died in 1972, my daughter in 1980, my father in 1982, my brother in 1985, my Patti O'Kat in 2000, my sister in 2001 and my son in 2005. I'll spare you the aunts, uncles and cousins list. Not everyone counts pets, but I do and they don't live as long as we live, regardless of the care we give to them.

The death of a loved one is not the only kind of loss that is life shattering. My divorce was very painful and frightening, and if you are raising children alone, it is lonely and draining. I lost precious time with my children for fun as well as for helping and supporting them. I lost our home, which we all loved.

After my husband and I separated, I struggled to hold things together without sufficient income, finishing a degree and trying to do the right things for two teenagers. The house needed work, the yard was going to seed, the children were acting out and I tried to manage crisis after crisis as they came at me. I felt completely drained and longed for somebody to turn to, someone who would listen to my problems and offer me support. I was lonely and carried the weight of the world on my shoulders.

Then, I met man who seemed to offer those things

to me and embarked on a nine year relationship that ended sadly. That was another life shattering loss to chalk up.

After Evie died, my faith, my view of life was rocked out of its foundations and I was adrift in a world that made no sense to me. I had been the best mother I knew how to be and I loved my children more than life. I was taught that if you were a good person, God would give you a good life, so I must be bad or that must be wrong. I tried on both ideas and decided that the part about God giving a good life to good people was wrong. There were other examples than mine, including victims of war, flood, famine, disease, crime, etc. I'll stop; it could be a very long list. Obviously, God just dropped us here and let us figure out how to roll with the punches if we could.

I was very angry with God, but I also felt that I was a very poor mother if this could happen to my child. She was beautiful and bright with multiple talents in music, art and poetry. She was a loyal friend and had a wonderful sense of humor. She was loving and affectionate with her family and friends; she was kind and always for the "underdog." She was so proud of her little brother and, although they would fight with each other, neither would tolerate an unkind word about the other. She was much more and she was only 18 years and 38 days old when she passed. So, I think, "If I had not gotten divorced from her father, if I had taken better care of her, etc., etc., etc."

Her death forced me to accept the realities that anything can happen, nothing is forever and you must make every day count. For me, that meant giving as much time and support to my boy and his family as possible, while working hard to secure my future; so that I would not become a burden to him as I would age. I am told that I spoiled both of them and maybe I did. It is possible that I would have made some different decisions with him if she had lived, but now I knew the fragility of life and happiness. Our lives would have been very different if she had lived. There is nothing as important as being there for the people you love and nothing worse than the regrets you may have if you lose them.

In time, I came to believe that "everything happens for a reason," that she is "in a better place" and that I had to "get on with my life." I stopped being angry with God and thanked him for 18 years and 38 days with her. I asked forgiveness for my shortcomings and accepted His grace. I miss her every day and will as long as I live, but I moved forward. I focused on a career, on my son, and later on his families; not necessarily in that order.

I should be getting proficient at managing losses, especially since the pace really picked up at the turn of the century. In 2000, I lost my Patti O'Kat after eighteen years of loving companionship. She was a pretty little calico, feisty, funny and smart. She trained me very quickly and we got along famously for eighteen years. She moved with me four times and always adjusted well. She liked our last house best, because it has a gas fireplace and she could lie in front of it on cold winter days. Nights were no problem; she snuggled with me and her purrrrs soothed me to sleep many an anxious or restless night.

In 2001, I lost my only sister and surviving sibling.

She was thirteen years older than me and was more like an extra parent than a sibling. That was the end of my family of origin. My nieces named me the Matriarch of the clan and I felt old. By now, my boy was married for the third time and very busy with his family.

When I returned from my sister's funeral, I was informed that my employment position was being eliminated, then that a new position was being created for me at a much lower salary: one third lower to be exact. Let nobody tell you that an undeserved demotion like that is not a loss. It does not compare with the loss of someone you love, but it does shake your confidence and image of yourself. I hung in for about a year at the lower position, partly because I needed major surgery and had good insurance, partly because I did not want to start a new job and quickly go out for a six week recovery period, and partly out of loyalty to my supervisor. I accepted the offer, had the surgery, and after a time, I knew that I had to leave. I was close to retirement age and the work I was doing was both boring and demoralizing. It was beginning to sink in that I was unlikely to get a decent job, regardless of my skills and track record, because of my age. I left anyway.

Shortly after I retired, I found that I needed another major surgery and went through with it in a very fatalistic frame of mind. I survived and the surgery was a success, which gave me a "second wind." I was beginning to rebuild and repopulate my life when the worst thing that could happen did.

My son and only surviving child died unexpectedly

at the age of 41. When he passed, I felt cut adrift in space. He had been my anchor to life, my reason for being. I knew that he would always need me if only because I was his mom. He loved me almost as much as I loved him and he told me so in many ways. It felt like I had outlived my life. Why was I here and what was the point? I did not see it and I felt disoriented and lost.

Knowing that anything could happen and nothing is forever did not make it any easier to accept his loss. Understanding something intellectually has nothing to do with accepting it emotionally. For years, I had been playing a game with God, "If you let me keep him, I will try to do everything right." I prayed for him every day and tried to support him as much as I could, leaving the rest to God and believing that God would not take him from me. I was wrong.

I was wrong for playing the game and even more wrong about prayer. Now, I know that prayer for others does not work. When someone prays for a certain outcome and gets it, they conclude that God answered their prayer. But, they seem to ignore the times when they don't get what they want and direct the cause to themselves or someone else. That is fine for them and it is comforting to believe that God can be persuaded to do what we want, but the obvious truth is that is not the case, nor should it be. God sees the whole picture; we do not.

My son's life and death were about him, not me. He died when he did because he needed to go then. Afterward, as I was reading some things he had written to me over the years and listening to some songs he gave me to listen to shortly before he died, I realized that he was trying to prepare me and that he knew his time was coming soon. I refused to pick up those hints and kept praying and affirming that he would recover from his physical problems and be well and strong again. I asked others to pray for him too and they did, but the only good it did was to bring me some peace of mind.

Yes, this is only my opinion based on my experience; but, there is biblical support for it. Christians are taught to pray by the example of The Lord's Prayer. Nowhere in The Lord's Prayer does it say anything about praying for others. It is all about your relationship to God.

> *"Our Father who art in Heaven,*
> *Hallowed be thy name.*
> *Thy kingdom come,*
> *Thy will be done*
> *In earth as it is in heaven.*
> *Give us this day*
> *Our daily bread*
> *And forgive us our debts*
> *As we forgive our debtors*
> *And lead us not into temptation,*
> *But deliver us from evil*
> *For Thine is the Kingdom*
> *And the power and the glory*
> *Forever. – Amen"*

When you "let go and let God," which is a very popular phrase, you are saying "Thy will be done." You are turning the decision over to him and that is as it should be. He sees the big picture and He knows best. So, what is the point of going to the Father to ask Him to change His mind? Why would we do that unless we were deluded into thinking that we know better than the Creator or that God would change the destiny of someone we love just because we ask? I was deluded, but now I see clearly and I accept it intellectually and emotionally.

That is what I have learned from the loss of my boy and with all the pain of missing him and the fear about being truly alone as I age, I must learn a new life. At the end of the day, we have to be about our own lives. I must find a way to manage the pain and find some joy. It is up to me to take care of myself as best I can and to help others when I see a need.

Life can be a hard school, but it is all we have and I continue to try to learn as much as possible this time around. Yes, I believe in reincarnation and that inspires me to try even harder to get it right this time. I know that my children are together and happy and that they have their pets with them. I "saw" them in my mind with their arms around each other, she holding my cat and his dog at her side, wagging his tail. They were so happy to be reunited and I know they will be glad to see me when I get there; and, I WILL get there.

But, it is not my time yet. There must be things undone that I need to do to complete my own life mission and I believe that it is my job to discover them and get them done. The discovery will come from prayer and meditation, from seeking direction from God. Getting them done is my part, so I will need to take care of myself and give it my best effort. I hope and pray that I am up to the task. Dr. Schuller of the *Hour of Power* says, "If God brings you to it, He will take you through it." I'm going forward with that thought.

A Cat

Sometimes, I wish I was a cat;
Sleep eighteen hours a day.
When I am sad that would be great.
It would all go away.

But, in good time I'd still awake
And my heart again would break.
Is that why, do you suppose,
The cats sleep on in sweet repose?

Perhaps, their little hearts broke too
And that is all they know to do
To get a break from pain and feeling,
A longing for which there is no healing.

Sleep on, my precious furry friend.
I hope your pain may sometime end
If pain it is that makes you sleep,
Not just the company you keep.

I know I cannot be a cat,
Not in this lifetime; that is that.
So other means I must employ
To find less grief and search for joy.

Albert's 19th birthday

Our Family Ends

In my family of origin, people stayed married. They "made their bed and they laid in it." I was the first to divorce and it shocked them. If my mother had been alive at that time, I don't know if I could have gone through with it. Mother died in April of 1972 and my husband and I separated in 1977.

Having spent some time studying the subject of families, in school and out, I concluded that we are likely to follow the pattern of our family of origin when we start our own family. To a great extent, I did this, but at the time, would have told you that I was doing things much differently. My parent's marriage bumped along, but there was little joy in it that I could see. Dad rarely did anything right, and when he would do a good thing, he was unlikely to get any credit for it. Mother's resentment of him was understandable; he had been unfaithful and been caught. They married in 1923 and he never held a steady job, except for the WPA during WWII, until 1945. He did not even take responsibility for chopping sufficient wood for the stoves that heated our old farmhouse. Even the farmhouse was a gift from his father. But, he kept the job he got in 1945 until retirement, and never missed a day.

So, when I thought about marriage, I was looking for someone who would work and provide a comfortable home for our family. Of course, I also wanted to fall in love and live happily ever after. I did fall in love and he did provide for most of the years of our marriage.

I had started college immediately after high school on a State of NY Regents Scholarship and not much more. Naturally, I had a summer job at the end of that second semester, but, I contracted infectious mononucleosis in a very serious way and was hospitalized. When I was released, the doctor's instructions were that I was to take off the fall semester and get my health back. I did that and when I felt better, I was incredibly bored. To make a long story short, I join the Women's Army Corps on February 20, 1959, and that is where I met my future husband.

He was handsome and fun, big and strong and he took charge. He was in the Military Police and I had some competition for his attention; he looked great in that uniform. He got orders to Korea and we decided to get married before his deployment, after knowing each other only three months. When he returned, we had the "honeymoon" at Fort Hood, Texas, his next duty station; and it did not take long for me to become pregnant. He was proud. I was delighted. The first years of the marriage were good, and when the problems began to grow, I became the "Queen of Denial." I would not look at what I did not wish to see, so I tried to pretend everything was fine for as long as I could convince myself.

Eventually, I could hide from the truth no longer and the situation was getting out of control. When the children got to middle school age, I decided to complete my education and find a job as a music teacher, which gave me the same hours as my children and a decent salary.

As a veteran, I had the GI Bill to pay the school and the plan was that the degree and a good job might give me the confidence to stand up to him. Maybe we could make things work if I was stronger and more self-sufficient. But things did not get better; they got worse, and the closer I came to getting the degree the harder it got for me, and the more our conflicts disturbed the children. Things finally came to a head in an argument that left him shaken and me emotionless. That night we agreed to separate and he left three days later for a job in another state.

I was now doing my student teaching. I had the GI Bill, I gave private voice and piano lessons to as many students as I could find, and I got a job as a student worker at the college library. I borrowed some money and somehow we got by. I needed to be with Albert and Evie more than I was able and it was hard on all of us. Still, I could not see a better life for us if I did not complete my education, and I was so close. I did what I thought was best and I did the best I knew to do.

We were each 20 years old when we married and, in so many ways, naïve. I tried to hold the family together, but in retrospect I now believe that it would have been better for all of us if we had separated sooner. The family I dreamed of ended in chaos, fear and sadness, but the worst was yet to come.

On February 7th of 1980, Evie was living with me, but staying with a school friend during the week to attend her high school; it was her senior year. Albert was living with his father, and he called me and said, "Mom, you need to get to the Atlantic City Medical Center as fast as you can. Something has happened to Evie." I got there as fast as I could, but it did not matter. When I walked up to the desk, I saw her name and DOA. I knew what that meant. My life went grey.

A complete autopsy was mandated, as it was considered an unattended death, but all they could find were the traces of a head cold, which she had the prior weekend. Of course, they were looking for drugs - she was a teenager. They found no traces at all, because she was not using drugs. The Death Certificate read "cardiac arrest" and when I asked the Medical Examiner to explain that to me, I was told that it was like an adult SIDS death and, although not common, there were several cases with that diagnosis in the county every year. I asked if she might have choked and if there was any sign that she struggled. I was told that it looked as if she had just laid down and went back to sleep; the covers were not disturbed. That was some comfort, but the big WHY remains to this day. I have accepted that it was God's plan for her and her time to go, but the medical reason will always be a question in my mind.

It took another two years for the divorce to be final, as there was a dispute over the division of property. Albert moved back in with me and brought one of his cousins with him for comfort and company. They both transferred to the school near me.

We received an invitation to what would have been Evie's graduation and we decided to attend in her honor. It was so hard to see her class out there in the field, tossing up their hats and hugging each other in joy and farewell as they began their adult lives. She had so looked forward to that day, but she did not live to enjoy it. Her graduation photo, in cap and gown, sits on the mantel in my home. Sometimes I move it to the piano, but it will never be put away in my lifetime.

I am so proud of her. Things were so difficult in the last years and she deserved so much better. She was highly intelligent, a fine musician and poet. She wrote songs and was an accomplished artist, working in oils, pencil and chalk. She had a beautiful speaking and singing voice and could harmonize to anything on the spot. She was affectionate and funny. She adored her cat, dog, guinea pig and rabbit. She was passionate about music, art, poetry, her family, her friends and animals in general. Evie was passionate about life. She was a beautiful person and a beautiful soul and I loved her so much.

Albert dropped out of school as soon as he reached the age where he could do so without parental consent; he could not deal with going back to the same school that they had attended together, but he wanted to be back with his old friends and his cousin, who had returned to his parent's home. For a time, Albert stayed with his aunt and uncle and then got a job and shared an apartment with his cousin. He later earned a GED and established a career, but he never recovered completely from the loss of his sister; neither did I.

NOTE: What follows is a poem that Evie wrote in 1979 when she was 17. She had been deeply in love and had begun to realize that it was not going to work out. What emotion is more intense than first love? We put the last line of this poem on her grave marker, "The rose needing only the sun's embrace to free it of the canvas." Albert and I discussed what to inscribe and he agreed that this was a good choice. He also added, "We miss you."

The Rose

The sun creeps up slowly to its fullness;
As I watch its reflection
In the water,
I see your face,
As the tears trickle down mine,
Like the paint on the picture of the rose
I'm finishing.

I remember summer days, and rain,
Talks we've shared,
The feeling I've kept.
A silent rose, reaching to the warmth,
No knowing if it will ever bloom,
But never dying.

Constant thoughts of you;
Your reflection in the lake
When the only one here is me.
Fantasies,
Making it possible
For warmth
In the winter's cold air.

Times the bud almost opened,
But the weeds
Blocked out the sunlight.
Tears and wishes,
The rose needing only the sun's embrace
To free it of the canvas.

Evie's graduation picture

All About Me
(or The Cheese Stands Alone)
June 2005

I gave myself away, always. Losing myself in a relationship was so natural and so comfortable, especially when it was a romantic relationship. I would become the perfect match for my chosen one and he would become my protector; except that I sometimes came to a point where I needed protection from him.

I have lost the people I loved most in my life and I am trying so hard to find a reason, some value to my life. Did I lose them because it is the only way that I may learn to be the person I would be if I did not give myself away? Life is not an easy school, nor gentle when we don't get the message.

There is a country song called Freedom's Just Another Word for Nothing Left to Lose. After my last heart rending loss, I think about this. Is this empty freedom the reward? It is true that my biggest worry is gone with him. My greatest fear was that I would lose a child and I have lost both of my children. I always tried to preserve family heirlooms and things they liked for them. After Evie died, it was all about Albert and those things I cherished would all go to him for distribution or for him to keep. Now what? I question if anybody else would want any of my little treasures. There is little of value and there may not be one member of the family who wants anything of mine, regardless of value. Why am I saving anything? I think I'll un-clutter and see what I can get out of my so called inheritance. I'll use the things I saved for company and I'll get rid of whatever I don't want to use. OK, that's a kind of freedom, a sad kind, but freedom nonetheless.

What else is freedom worth to me? My financial position prevents me from doing much travel, which I would enjoy, but who would be my travel companion? Do I want to travel alone? I have done it and could do it again if I can find a way to pay for it. I don't have to pretend to be anything I'm not ever again. I can be as eccentric as it occurs to me to be without fear of embarrassing anybody but myself.

There are people who love me and whom I love, and someone might be there if I need help. There are people who will care when I die, but my absence won't cause the pain it would have caused my children. No lives will be disrupted by my loss except that of my cats, if they survive me. Yes, it is all about me at last.

When I was contemplating retirement, it seemed to me to be a new beginning and I was not sure what I could or should do with it. For years before the projected retirement date, I had sensed that big changes were coming in my life. I thought it was mostly about retirement, but what evolved proved retirement to be a very small piece of the picture.

Retirement came on sooner than planned. When companies change hands, they are very creative about encouraging those they want to leave. I was a bit de-motivated when they cut my salary by a third, moved me into a tiny office and gave me work I could do in my sleep, while someone with no experience moved into my office and took over my department.

Things got a bit dicey for me when I needed surgery, not once but twice in the next two years. Someone who lives alone faces challenges when they are sent home from major surgery, but I coped and decided that this would give me more time to contemplate my new life.

The events mentioned above were a walk in the park compared to what followed. One of the perks I saw in retirement was more time to spend with my son and his family, and that was true for a time. Then I got the early morning call on a cold, snowy January morning. There was no need to rush, because it was already too late.

I am still in the stage of grief where I can get really annoyed and angry with people complaining because they think they might die. Dying is not the worst thing that can happen to you. Losing your reasons to live is right up there with the worst. Losing your health certainly contends and not having enough resources for physical comfort would qualify.

Evie did not live long enough to attend the much anticipated high school graduation or go to college or marry or have children. Al had a lucrative career, married and had children. She missed out on so much and he left so much behind, but each died during sleep and that is some comfort to me. They did not die in pain or fear; they just went to sleep.

I mentioned that my boy married and had children, but I only referred once to his having married three times. He had a daughter with his first wife and a son with his second wife. The third marriage produced two step children for him, and the second marriage had produced one; so, he left five children behind who loved him, as well as his parents and his wives. I still cannot understand why someone who was so loved and so needed should die while I, at my age and needed only by the cats, should live.

Now, where does that leave me in my new life? I still live alone, if you don't count the cats, who should be counted. I have some wonderful friends. My health is now pretty good, given my age; I love my home and my independence.

I still don't know what I want to be "when I grow up," but it is helping me think and heal to put these thoughts on paper. I read, I pray and I meditate. I go to the gym where I lift weights, walk and ride a stationary bike. I do lunch with my friends and belong to several organizations. I cry and cry some more. I drink more wine and eat more cheese than is good for me and I gain weight.

On the days I don't cry, I feel "born again;" free to be myself for myself at last. I am more relaxed with my friends and family and more inclined to say what I think and ask for what I need than I ever was. This is as new for them as it is for me and I hope they can accept it.

After thinking about being totally free, I feel guilty; then sad and I cry.

Given that everything passes, good and bad, I

guess this will too; but, it is a time of disorientation and confusion, of feeling like a split personality sometimes, and of struggle to find that "new normal" they talk about.

This is still the year of firsts without him: first Valentines Day, first Easter, first Mother's Day, first Father's Day, first 4th of July, first birthday, first Thanksgiving, first Christmas, first New Year and, finally, first one of my birthdays without him since his birth. Next year, I'll have some practice with each of those days and the pain will be a little less severe and a little less frequent. Ask me how I know? Somehow, I'll get through the firsts and move on to the seconds and somehow I'll learn to live a new way. Someday...

Albert and Evie, age 1 and 3

This Too Shall Pass

This too shall pass;
The good and bad.
Some things bring joy
Some make us sad.

We can't control
The quirks of fate, so
We put things on hold
And wait and wait.

And yet, there is
Another choice.
Think of good things
And rejoice.

Know sad times will go
As part of the flow
For a very good reason;
All things have a season.

Evie and Mom at the Mall

Albert and Mom at the Mall

Shadows on My Heart

"I'll be fine, Mom. I just have a slight cold. I'll watch TV for a while and go to bed early." It was a Saturday night in January 1980 and I had to go to work. Evie had come up for the week-end, as usual; but, she was sniffling and sneezing and a little feverish. She usually went with our little group, a trio, dancing and having a great time, but not tonight. She was wrapped up in a blanket on the sofa with a box of tissues and a glass of orange juice. I agreed with her plan, gave her the number of the club where we were working and told her to turn off the TV and get in bed no later than 11:00. She agreed and went back to watching the TV show. How much I would have preferred to stay in and "baby" her, but I had promised to do this job, I knew she would be all right and I would have let the employer and my musician friends down if I had not held up my end of the deal.

It had been a really nice day. This morning, she had asked me to dry her hair after she took a shower. I had not done that in a long time and had delighted in toweling those beautiful blond curls while we talked. She was worried about graduation and about funding for college and many other things, so we talked about them and I tried to reassure her that we would get it all worked out; then we planned our day. We were soon off to the mall for some shopping. It was like old times.

So, I hugged and kissed her and, reluctantly, went to work. We performed until 1:00 a.m. on Saturday nights, so it was after 2:00 when we got home to find Evie wrapped up on the sofa watching TV. I scolded her for not being in bed and asleep as she had agreed, but did not really have the heart to push it. She was just a couple of weeks past her eighteenth birthday and old enough to know what she needed to do. She said that she had gone to bed, but a coughing spell woke her up and she thought watching TV would make her sleepy. I could understand that, but chased her back upstairs, gave her some more cough syrup and tucked her into her bed.

It was so great to tuck her into her bed in her room again and I treasured the moment. I felt sad that she did not live with me all the time, but knew that I might as well become accustomed to that; she would graduate in June and then be off to college. She might choose to go to a school nearby and live with me or she might not. She was eighteen!

A few days later, I was taking down what remained of the Christmas decorations and trying to decide what should go on the mantle in place of the Nativity set when Albert called. The man I hoped to marry was with me when the call came in and we left immediately for the drive to the hospital.

It was one of the two longest rides of my life, although it only took 45 minutes. When I went to the registration desk at the emergency room, I looked at the sign up sheet and saw her name with DOA next to it. It did not seem real and I did not believe it. I told them who

I was and the nurse escorted us to a small room, where I found Albert waiting for me. I looked into his eyes and went into his arms. It was real and he was only sixteen years old.

The nurse urged me into a chair and we sat down. I asked Albert what he knew and he told me that Stephanie, the girl Evie had been staying with during the week, had called him after the ambulance took Evie to the hospital. The high school was on split sessions and Evie and Stephanie were on the later session. Stephanie had called Evie at the usual time to get up for breakfast, but Evie asked her to call her again in an hour, because she was so tired. She had been at a rehearsal for an upcoming show at the high school the night before and they had practiced late. They had also eaten dinner after that and she was not hungry; she needed the extra sleep more than breakfast. Stephanie said "fine" and went to get her own breakfast. When she returned to wake Evie in an hour, she would not wake up. Stephanie had learned CPR and applied it to Evie with no response. She called 911 and they responded quickly, but none of their efforts made any difference. She was gone.

When the doctor came in to talk to us, I asked if she might have choked in her sleep, thinking of the cold she had the prior week-end. I wanted to know if she had been in pain of any kind. I was told that was not the case; that the EMTs found her laying there exactly as she was when Stephanie left her, with bed clothes undisturbed, as if she were sleeping. She was a healthy eighteen-year-old girl, full of energy and enthusiasm. It did not make any sense.

My fiancé, who had driven me to the hospital, was urging me to leave, and there was nothing else to be done. Evie had been identified and the rest was out of our hands.

I asked Albert to come with me, but he did not feel that he could do that, as he had not yet told his father and felt that he needed to do that now. He was sixteen years old and took on the job of telling his parents that his sister was dead. His heart was breaking, but he did not cry. He hugged me hard, told me he would call me later, got out of the car and walked up to his father's house. We waited until he waved us away from the door and went in.

Baby Brother

Another day's dawning;
I'm thinking of you.
How I miss looking into
Your cute eyes of blue.

It's been way too long
Since we last saw each other.
Wish that I saw you more,
Cause you're my baby brother.

Okay, you're no baby,
But you're little to me.
Yes, Albert, I know
You're a whole six foot three.

Well, until our fates bring us
Together again,
Know that I love you
As my brother and friend.

Evie wrote this in 1979 during a period when Albert was living
with me and she was with her Dad.

Evie at 17

Dark Days

After leaving Albert with his father, we drove back the route we had come, but nothing was the same. We did not talk much and I don't remember if I cried or not; actually, I don't remember much of the ride except that we did not talk much.

My fiancé took me directly to my family doctor for medication and the doctor shared that he had also lost a daughter. That was, somehow, comforting. How awful to be comforted by knowing that someone else has suffered such a loss. He showed me a painting of her on his office wall and my thought was that she was young when he lost her; he did not have as much to forget. I hurt too much to realize then that neither did he have as much to remember.

We went home and I dutifully took my pill and lay down on the sofa, trying to absorb what had happened, but I could not. My mind just kept going in circles, remembering every one of our last conversations and every comment she made to examine them for clues. Then it went back in time. Was this a latent result of a concussion she got when she was away at summer camp at the age of ten? She had fallen out of the top bunk on her head and it was a serious concussion. Or, was it the concussion she got when riding in the back of her father's truck with her brother and some other children? A driver had cut us off, causing us to slam on the brakes. She was sitting next to the cab and hit her head hard. Back in the 60's it was not uncommon for children to ride in the back of a truck on a summer day, especially if you lived in a rural area, and we did. Now, I am appalled that we permitted it, but it seemed just to be fun for them at the time and he was driving carefully.

Maybe it was not from a concussion, maybe it was a latent bacteria of some kind. She had been in hospital when she was very young with a very high fever for which the cause was never found. She had been sick many times as she was growing up. How could I know what might have caused her death? There was no sense to be made of it and I could not continue to lie on that sofa any longer. The TV was on, but it was so irrelevant; who cared? What difference did the weather make or the news of robberies and accidents, much less health reports?

It sounds trite to say that I could not understand how everything continued as usual, but that is how I felt. My world was indeed "upside down" and I knew nothing would ever be the same.

I wondered how Albert was managing with his father and I just wanted him with me. I needed to see him, hear him and touch him to be sure I still had him, but his father needed him too and I would have to wait for that relief.

Finally, it occurred to me that I needed to call my family and tell them what had happened, but I dreaded that so much. That would make it real. I know that my fiancé called our friends and would have called my family for me, but I needed to do it myself and I started by calling my sister. My mother was dead but my Dad lived with her and she would tell him. I made the call. I remember asking my sister to tell the rest of the family, but I don't remember much else about our conversation except that they would be on their way as soon as possible.

I could not think of anything else to do. I could only lie back down on the sofa and go through all of the potential causes over her lifetime, over and over again.

What could have caused her to die? She was fine when I spoke to her two days before; she was so excited about a concert that she would be part of and a party that she and some friends were throwing for a beloved teacher who was moving out of the area. When I hung up the phone from that last phone call, I sighed with a combination of happiness and exhaustion. She had so much energy that I got tired just listening to her sometimes. I immediately felt guilty for that thought.

Then, I returned in my mind to the weekend before, when I had put her on a bus to go back to where she was attending high school. This was a first, as I usually drove her there, but there was a bad snow storm and I am not the best driver under those conditions. I thought she would be safer in the bus; I did not trust myself to make the long drive successfully. While waiting at the bus stop, we went into a little coffee shop to get hot chocolate, because it was so cold outside and we had some time. We were giggling about a man in the coffee shop who was flirting with both of us. I went out with her as soon as we saw the bus, we hugged and kissed and I told her "Take good care of my girl." She promised and climbed onto the bus. I stood on the curb to see her off and, as she turned to wave to me, I saw tears in her eyes. There was nothing I could do but throw a kiss and wave as the bus pulled away from the stop. She called me when she got in to let me know she had gotten there safely and she sounded happy and tired, so I did not bring up the tears that I saw. I thought to save my questions for her next visit, but that visit was not to be and I will never know.

Did she have a premonition that she would not see me again? I had no such thought at the time.

She had always been very psychic; actually, both of my children had strong psychic abilities. One of the tricks that they liked to play on me was to cause me to change the radio station in the car. I liked the "oldies" and they liked contemporary rock and roll. They would be together in the back seat and I would have my favorite station on the radio until, at some point, I would decide to check out some other stations. Oddly, we would then be listening to contemporary rock and when I realized what I was hearing, I would look into the back seat to see both of them grinning at me. Of course, there were loud complaints when I changed it back. This happened many times and Evie told me that she was sending me messages "Change the station.", "This is good, keep this one on." etc.

They called our yellow Mercury Comet "The Yellow Submarine," and we would sing that song loudly whenever we thought of it while driving along. We had fun together.

But, back to that night; did she know? I had set up an appointment with the family doctor that weekend, because she told me that she was not feeling just right. There was nothing specific that she could tell me; she just did not feel quite right. She was due for a gynecological exam, so I thought we should start there and set it up; but she did not live long enough to see that doctor. She was so upbeat most of the time that I did not think there was anything seriously wrong, but maybe she was putting on a good front to keep me from worrying about her. It is entirely possible.

We got nothing from the autopsy; they could not find a reason for her death. In later years, I read about Sudden Arrhythmia Death Syndrome (SADS) and it seems to me that is a likely cause. Since it can be passed down in families, I asked Albert to get checked and have his children checked. He did that, but did not go to one of the specialists in the field, so, I was never really confident that he had the most accurate result. However, that was as far as he would go with it and that was not the cause of his death.

The family gathered and we got through her funeral and burial. My memories are hazy, except for the sight of Evie in the coffin with the blue silk lining and a few incidents that startled me. One of those was of my lawyer, who had stood by me through everything, like a protective mother figure. She said, "You don't have to be a hostess." It had not occurred to me that was what I was doing; I just felt it was my job to greet people who came to me and to thank them for being there for us. Also, it distracted me from thinking that I would have to leave her here and never see her again.

I could not bear for the casket to be closed. I had never seen enough of that lovely face and if she had lived to be 100 years of age, I would still not have seen enough of her. The Funeral Director had to decide which parent was to leave first, since we were not together, and he chose me. I'm sure it seemed logical to him, since her father paid his bills, but my heart broke when I walked out of that room, knowing that I would never see her face again and that I would not have the privilege of tucking her in one last time.

She was laid to rest next to her paternal grandparents in a country cemetery near where she grew up; that was what she would have wanted. Leaving her there in the ground in that cold cemetery was something I could not have done if others were not leading me away.

I lived some distance from there, but I was incapable of putting on any kind of funeral reception afterward anyway. One of Evie's best friends opened her family's home to all of us and provided a buffet after we returned from the cemetery. Being with her friends was probably the best for me. That is another part of the story that I can't give you any details about, because I remember so little of it. I remember my gratitude to Donna for the reception, I remember some of the people who attended, but that is the extent of my recall of the event. How much of my failed memory resulted from the medication I was taking and how much from the shock, I will never know and it does not matter now as it did not matter than.

We went home and I went upstairs to her room, where I sat on the side of the bed where I had sat last

Sunday to brush her hair. I could smell her scent in the room and then I cried as I had never cried before.

Evie and her dog Abby

Mom
by EvieG - 1979

A long time ago, I met a girl
Who looked a lot like me.
Like childhood friends we dreamed and planned
Of how our lives would be.

Life seemed to look us in the eyes,
Throwing all its pain.
We held each other through the storms;
Together faced the rain.

Then time arranged to have things changed;
We turned to different friends.
We learned a lot about ourselves,
But our bond refused to end.

Then one day we met again
And looked inside each other.
The things I saw were beautiful
In my best friend, and my mother.

Imagine If You Dare

Imagine, if you dare, that your marriage is over (divorce or death), your parents are dead, your siblings are dead and your children are dead. Your grandchildren are in the care of the spouses of your children, but you are not really part of their lives. They are kind and you are always made welcome. They remember you on holidays. They are loving and considerate, but the grandchildren are growing up or grown up; they don't need you for anything anymore. You are 67 years old and no longer employed. What would you do?

This is my dilemma. Maybe, I could get a job; my health is quite good for my age. I could look for a husband or companion; men are being divorced and widowed all the time. (What are the odds of success at either of these endeavors for a shy, chubby, 67-year-old woman?) Or, I can continue on the path I began when I retired: walk with friends, exercise at the health club, attend meetings of various social groups, volunteer for worthy causes, read, write, whatever it pleases me to do. But there was one activity that stabilized everything else and that has been struck from the list that made up my retirement path. That activity was time with my family, both on holidays and any other day we chose. I no longer have a family.

As I write this, it is nearing the end of the first year without my Al and the dreaded Holiday Season is upon me. I cannot imagine sitting down to a Thanksgiving dinner without him. He was the focus of my Thanksgiving for 41 years and I can't look around that table and not see his smiling face. Friends and family members have invited me to share the holiday with them, but I just want to hide out in my refuge with my cats and pretend it is any other day. It is possible that I will give in and accept an invitation, but it is equally possible that I will be a "wet blanket" if I do and I will certainly be more stressed in that situation. What to do? Will I hurt the feelings of loving, caring people if I opt out? Can I expect them to understand? Who can understand if they have not walked in my shoes? Who dares to imagine what it would be like?

Sounds like a pity party, doesn't it? I know that I am not the only one in this position, and I know how fortunate I am to have been invited to share Thanksgiving with others who know that I will be a cloud on their holiday. Further, I know and count my blessings: my faith, my health, my remaining extended family, my finances, my comfortable home, my mobility, my cats and I could go on. I have many good things in my life, but I no longer have a family of my own and I have discovered that, regardless of whoever else is in my life, I feel totally alone without my son. I know that is not reality, but it is real in my heart.

As if Thanksgiving is not enough, there is Christmas looming on the horizon. There is NO WAY to avoid the commotion Christmas creates in shops, on TV, etc. It is impossible to get away from it and I am having no part of it this year. Last year, I bought one of those new pre-lit trees. I don't have much room for a tree and I found a slim one at the right price and enjoyed it immensely. I was once a "Christmas" person and loved everything about the season. Now, it is the season I dread the most.

If/when I survive Christmas, I get to face New Year's Eve and day. I have lots of experience with managing New Year's Eve; it was my daughter's birthday and I lost her 25 years ago. New Year's Day is another story; that was MY holiday. My son always wanted to have holidays at his house, but New Year's Day was never one they chose to celebrate, because they were too tired from New Year's Eve. I also got to do Easter dinner, as they did a big brunch and Easter egg hunt when the children were small, so those were My holidays. I expect that I can ignore New Year's Day without much interference; nobody pays much attention to that anymore, do they? And I'll find a way to deal with Easter too.

The advice I get is that I must look ahead and not behind and I know that is right. Maybe next year....

Maybe next year, I will dare to imagine my future. Maybe next year, I will be able to evaluate the options and make some decisions about the "new" direction for my life. Maybe next year, I will be able to face the dreaded Holiday Season with some grace and feel that I am some kind of asset in the lives of those I love. This year, I will keep putting one foot in front of the other, I'll cry whenever I need to and I'll try to support my loved ones as best I can and pray that they will understand when I can't.

Can you imagine? Do you want to? I did not dare to imagine what this would be like and that was just as well. I could not have faced knowing that the last time that I saw him or spoke to him would be the last time.

A few years ago, I bought a small sign at a craft fair which said, "It can happen." I bought it because I wanted to be reminded that anything can happen. Being an optimist by nature, I was thinking "anything good." A woman who was behind me in the checkout line said, "That is SO true. Anything can happen. One of us could get killed in a car accident on the way home today." I thought that was an awful way to look at life, but now I finally can see "anything" as having two sides. The sign is still hanging on my wall in the hall upstairs in an attempt to keep me level-headed.

I do believe that everything happens for a reason and I don't expect to understand; but, I will go on in faith, and somehow get through this year of "firsts." My mantra is "Let go and let God." Without my faith, I could not have come this far; and with His guidance, I hope to find my way into my future. I know that it is up to me to make decisions and act on them. Divine guidance is just that; the work is up to me. I don't know if I am strong enough to make something useful of what remains of my life, but I know that I must imagine my tomorrow before I can claim it and I must give it my best.

Lost in Memory
1979 by EvieG

Don't let the faraway look,
Sometimes found in my eyes,
Scare you, 'cause I'm just thinking,
Deep inside of my mind.

If I seem to be lost,
When you look at my face,
I am just deep in thought;
From this world I've escaped.

I can hold conversation
If you wish or I will,
But my heart isn't in it,
Lost in memory still.

Some will call it day dreaming;
I say abstract thought,
'Cause it gives me the answers
To questions long sought.

Ms. Starr Cat (above); Dr. Smudge (below)

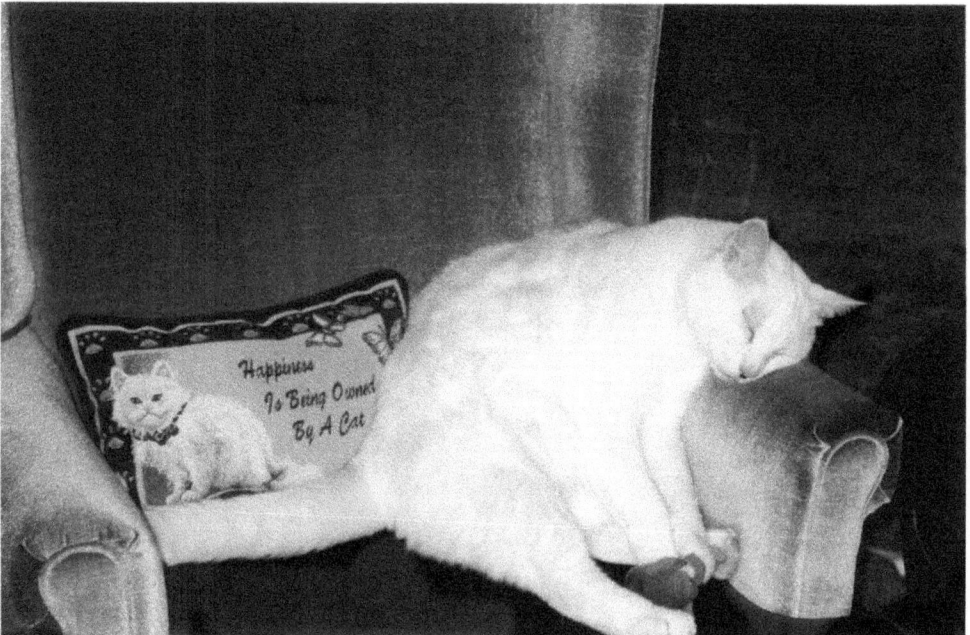

Chill Wind
Winter 2006

I forgot; I totally forgot. The wind is whipping my hair out of its fasteners and making my ears almost numb. This is GREAT! I have not done this in such a long time that I did not even remember that I love walking in the wind, especially a chill wind. It is invigorating, bracing, and energizing.

As I round the circle and start in the opposite direction, the wind whips my hair into my face, so I begin to fumble for the hood on my jacket. Better! I tuck in the hair and that works for about 30 seconds, then I begin to dig for the strings that tie on the hood and once that is done, it feels great again.

"I'm gonna' get some life back into my life." The refrain from *Hello Dolly* keeps running through my head and I keep pace with it. Can I really do that? Get some life back? Today, it seems possible.

This is my first attempt in thirteen months to walk in between my exercise sessions, so I don't want to overdo it, but I am tempted to go around again just for the pure joy of it. As I near the end of the lap, I decide that was not a good idea, given what I want to do when I get home today, so I take my handbag out of the trunk of my car and get into the driver's seat. Looking in the mirror, I decide that I will wear a hat for my errands; there is no hope for the hair and I might get arrested if I go into a shop with that hood on.

When I open the front door of my home, the quiet envelopes me in sharp contrast with the blow outside, just as the warmth penetrates my skin and comforts me. Home is good. Even the cats are sleeping, so I'll just fix some lunch and get on with the day.

Thirteen months ago, I lost my reason for living. There was nothing I wanted to do and nowhere I wanted to go, except to follow my children; but I could not add to the trauma of others by taking my life and I am not that sure about the afterlife that I am willing to take the chance of going to an unwanted destination.

What a surprise to feel some anticipation and hope for the future. I am not sure what I have to do to get some life back into my life, but I think I am ready to try. I know the tears are not over and that they may never be over for me, but that does not mean that I can't find some happiness.

By mid-afternoon, I am in tears again.

Before I can tell you this little story, you need to know two things about me. The first is that I am a "cat lady." I have two beautiful, wonderful felines in my home and life, and I treat them like family, which they are to me. Second, I believe in spirits and I do not fear them; I encourage them and I sometimes feel surrounded by them.

Now, I can proceed. My eighteen pound white male cat (Dr. S) is the baby of our little family. He follows me ceaselessly and, when I am away from home, he sleeps on a window ledge to watch for me most of the time. My little black beauty (Ms. S.) is all feline. She is a great cricket hunter and bird terrorizer. She can't get at them, because she can't go outside, but she hides in her "blind" and pounces on the glass when they come to eat at the feeder outside the window.

She has decided to sleep all afternoon, being exhausted from her exertions of the morning. I go upstairs to make up the bed with clean sheets and the white cat runs after me, passes me and hops onto the bed, all the while purring and squeaking in his inimitable way. Ok, I tell him, "I'll get the robe and tuck you in." Ever since I have had him, he has loved to be "tucked in" to my bathrobe. It is thick terrycloth and I make a circle of it on the bed, in which he curls up to take his nap. He will need to wash himself first, of course, but even before that I must lie down beside him and let him knead my arm, or leg, or whatever body part he can reach while he purrs contentedly. When he gets tired of kneading, he wraps a paw or two around my arm and snuggles down. He was lying there, purring and squeaking, and being even more affectionate than usual, so I decided to sing him a lullaby to see if that would make him sleepy. It worked on my children.

What was I thinking? I began to sing him the songs I sang to them and he did love it. His eyes went shut and the purring got softer, but I was being flooded with memories. When I sang my son's favorite, "Little Man," that polished me off and I cried and cried. My little boy always asked for "Little Man," which was short for "Little Man, You've Had a Busy Day" and was popular in the 20's or 30's (if ever). It was a piece of music my mother had collected and given to me and it was a lullaby, so I used it. I loved to sing to my babies. The last line of it was, "Time you should be dreaming, little man, you've had a busy day." My little feline buddy continued to comfort me with his cuddles and purrs and I was grateful for them; it always helps, but I was seeing my baby boy's little face, drifting off to sleep while I finished the song and remembering that he did not wake up from his last sleep.

Finally, I knew I had to get on with my plans for the day and went downstairs to get started, leaving Mr. Cat taking that bath in order to get down to some serious napping. I was busily dusting things and putting them on the dining room table in preparation for dusting the furniture and I was thinking about what I wanted to get done with the rest of the day when I heard Albert's voice say "Hi Mom." I saw nothing and the voice was soft, but it was very clear and it was his voice. It made me cry at the same time it comforted me.

Later, I went back upstairs with some clean laundry and found that a photo of him (which I keep in my bedroom), had been laid down on the window sill face up. My first thought was to wonder if a cat knocked it over, but that was not possible. Both cats had been asleep from the time I went downstairs, leaving the picture standing up on the window ledge where I had put it. It was placed between a small container and a picture of his sister and it did not fall off the sill; it just lay there neatly in place. Furthermore, the window ledge is narrow, a typical window ledge. If it had been a cat, the picture would have fallen to the floor simply from the relative size of the ledge and the frame, and the cats never go to that part of the sill because they know they can't fit between the pictures.

Albert was here with me today. I have no doubts. When I told a therapist about the incident, she asked me if Albert had liked to play little tricks on me, and he did. Teasing me was one of his life's pleasures. I think that he made this visit to me because his spirit was so happy to see me enjoying that walk in the chill wind this morning that he wanted me to know how he felt and that he wants me to be happy again.

I did most of what I planned to do and decided to lie down for a few minutes, as I was short of sleep and beginning to feel it. I dropped off quickly and when I adjusted my position in my sleep, I had a strong sense of my mother's presence, as if she was watching over me as I slept.

Are you thinking that I spend too much time alone with the cats and that I imagine people around me to keep me company? I expect that you could make a case for that; but that would not make it true. I spoke to people in the park and in the shops and three people called me during the course of the day; they were all lengthy phone calls. I was not isolated, nor was I making things up in my imagination.

Tonight, I am writing this for two reasons; one is to sort it out for myself and the other is to share it sometime with someone who has lost a most precious love too.

I feel a poem stanza coming on. Sorry, but it must be said.

Today has been a special day,
And I've said all I have to say.
Doubt or believe, it's up to you;
But, trust yourself in all you do.

I thought that was all I had to say, but after reading it again, I have something to add. We had some tough times during the period when the father of my children and I were divorcing. It was heart-wrenching for the children and for me on their behalf and my own.

And I have to tell you something else about me: I am a packrat. I have saved papers from my birth forward to today. Recently, I have been sorting through files, purging things that should have been purged years ago, and generally trying to put my affairs in order. In a book, I found two letters that my son had written to me during that difficult time, and I had not been able to part with them. Last night, I wanted to talk to him about them, but he was gone.

I have framed an email message that he sent to me three years ago, telling me how much he loved me in such a beautiful way. He included a photo of him with the email and, before I acted on the letters, I talked to his picture on the email about the content of the letters. I told him that I was sorry if I had not always understood or if I had not always made the best decisions. I told him how much I always loved him and how much I miss him and then I burned the letters. I felt better afterward.

After writing about today, I remembered last night

and I think it is all part of the same experience. I reached out to him and his spirit came and stayed with me today to let me know that he forgives my weaknesses, as I must do if I am to find happiness again, and that is what he wants for me.

How blessed I have been to have had such children.

Christmas morning

Borrowed Blessings

It's not supposed to be this way, everybody knows.
You raise your children lovingly; your pride just grows and grows.
Then, one day you get a call, "Get here quick, OK?"
You rush to Emergency. You see the DOA.

This just can't be happening.   I'll wake up from this dream.
It's all just too surreal. It can't be what it seems.
The sun comes up, the moon goes down, and they do it in
reverse.
The seasons change and holidays feel mostly like a curse.

And so the years go by and by; grandchildren ease the pain.
I am still blessed. I have him and, I feel joy again.
Life has a rhythm and life goes on, I watch grandchildren grow.
I see the pride he takes in them and remember long ago.

Then, one day another call, "Get here quick, OK?"
I cannot move as fast this time and what for anyway?
They are gone, but not forgotten; nor, ever will they be
By those who loved with all their hearts those they can no longer
see.

I've had some time to think on this and this is what I know;
Each was a borrowed blessing and each one had to go.
I do not know or understand the reason for my losses;
God is good and wise and kind; but, all must bear our crosses.

God knows that I am grateful to have had her eighteen years;
And, for having him for forty-one in spite of all the tears.
There is comfort when I know that his children bloom and grow.
And, I feel sure that he will see and he will watch them as they
go.

So, I thank God for all my life, for blessings I receive,
And seek to find His plan for me; and, hope, although I grieve.
He must have one that I can find, so I am sure to be
Worthy when my life is done; then, my loved ones I will see.

Albert and his red Firebird

Messages from Evie

One great comfort to me is that I feel that the spirits of my children remain close to me and they can be quite creative about delivering their messages when they want to get in touch.

Shortly after Albert moved into the apartment with me in 1984, I came home from work one day to see a piece of folded paper on the divider between the dining room and kitchen. I picked it up, thinking that he had left me a message, but what I saw on the paper was, "I love you. Evie." I did not believe my eyes and when I looked at it again and more closely, it said, "I love you. Cindy." Al's girlfriend must have given him the note or left it there before she went home on the previous night; but, I know what I saw when I picked it up and I had not been thinking about Evie when I came in. I was feeling sad and lonely about my new job, where I had not yet gotten to know the people or the job very well. This type of message seems to come when I need it most.

A few years later, I came home from work in a similar state of mind. The company that I had been part of had been sold and I was, once again, starting over with a new company. I was feeling the same sense of frustration at learning a new job and new culture while trying to find my place in it. I needed confidence and encouragement, but for all that Patti O'Kat (my calico fur ball) could give me, she could not give me those things, and there was nobody around who could.

At times like that, I missed Evie very much, because I knew we would have been cheerleaders for each other. I felt a compulsion to read the note that Evie had written on the back of the little photo she had given me for my wallet during her senior year. It never got to the wallet, because I cut it out for a locket that she and Al gave me for Christmas that year. I saved the part I cut off, though, and decided to piece the photo together and read her message to me again. I went directly to my bedroom and jewelry box and took the locket out. When I opened it, the photo was turned over with the message facing up. I took out the border that I had laid underneath it and read her words again. She had written, "Thanks for being you and for caring. I am proud of you and you are my best friend. You are one of a kind and I love you." After a good cry, I felt better and put the locket carefully away with the photo facing up. Her words still had the power to comfort and encourage me.

I had not turned over the photo in the locket and I know that Al would never go into my jewelry box; but even if he did, he would not have turned over her photo. The only way I could explain it was that her spirit wanted me to know that she was there and that she meant those words even now. I felt her spirit near me so often, and sometimes I would turn my head to speak to her before I remembered that she was not there. The presence of her loving spirit was always comforting to me.

Driven
1979 by EvieG

Live life to the fullest,
An old one once said.
Become part of your music;
Feed it into your head.

Push your mind to the end;
Just let yourself loose.
Thank God for your fingers
And their heavenly use.

Hail Hendrix for creating
The electric guitar,
Merging bare minds with metal;
Thanks to music, we are.

We've got to get into
The things we want most.
Got to keep living,
Got to learn how to coast.

To me, music is life.
It's the thing I live for;
I'm swallowed up in it
And I still crave for more.

Patti O'Kat

Patti O'Kat

The rain was coming down so hard that I could not see to drive and had to pull over to the side of the road to wait for it to let up. It was almost as dark as night, except for the flashes of lightening that accompanied the storm. I was returning home after taking flowers to Evie's grave for Memorial Day. I had lunch with an old friend afterward and the afternoon was turning into evening before I realized the time; in fact, it was the darkening sky that brought it to my attention.

It was summer of 1984 and I had just moved into my apartment; Al had not yet decided to join me, so nobody was home except my little calico cat. She was a stray that I adopted in Georgia and brought home with me and the apartment was yet another change in her short little kitty life, so I was worried about her. She had always been afraid of thunderstorms and tended to hide under furniture if I was not cuddling her.

This was the first time in my life that I had been truly alone. I had always had family or shared a residence, but now it was just Patti and me. As soon as I could see well enough to drive, I started heading home again as fast as I felt safe to do. When I arrived at the apartment, everything was totally dark; the power was out in the neighborhood. I was nervous in addition to being worried about my little Patti. I hoped I could remember where I had stashed the candles when I moved. I had a small flashlight in my purse, keyhole size, but better than nothing, and I found Patti asleep on the sofa. When I went to check on her she stretched and began to purr; she was fine. Then, I located candles and we got on with our evening, but it was like a sign to me. She had always been terrified in a storm and I was rather nervous about them myself, but she was fine and to my amazement, so was I, in spite of the awful drive home and the lack of power in a new apartment by ourselves. Patti and I turned a corner that night.

The lights soon came back on, and as I prepared for work the next day, I recognized that work was the main thing in my life now, after Albert. He still needed me from time to time, and probably always would, but he was pretty much his own man and that was as it should be. I decided to focus my energies on my work and see what I could make of my life from there that night.

Patti was my trusted confidant for eighteen years. She greeted me at the door when I came home from work every day, she snuggled under a blanket with me when I was sad or sick, she made me laugh with her antics and she let me know when it was time to go to bed every night by staring at me and meowing loudly. When I would start for the bedroom, she would run ahead of me and jump on the bed where she slept next to me every night.

When I lost Patti at the age of eighteen (which is a pretty good age for a cat), I vowed never to have another pet. It hurt too much to lose her and I gave away all of her things; she had quite a collection. I called the friend who stayed with her when I traveled for business or pleasure and gave her everything. She could barely get it all in her car. I told myself that I wanted to be free to travel without worrying about a cat and as I was approaching retirement, I did not need the expenses or restrictions or worries that accompany being owned by a cat. I was catless for a year when Al remarried and his new wife had two beautiful cats. Al's allergies took a turn for the worse and his asthma returned; it had to be the cats. So, when his wife told me that she would have to find a home for them and that they must go as a set, I would not have let anybody else have them; I already loved them.

Now, I have two lovely cats in my home and gladly spend whatever is needed on them. My trips are rare and the cost is not exorbitant.

Considering what they give me, it is the best deal I could make. After losing Al, I saw no reason to get up in the morning, but a hungry cat will convince you that getting up and feeding him or her is VERY important. And, because of them, I can smile in the morning instead of lying there and missing my boy.

When I wake up, Al is my first thought just as he is my last thought when I go to sleep. They pull me back into the day, into my life and theirs, and at night, they purr and snuggle with me, which comforts and soothes me into sleep. They are my sleeping pills and they are my alarm clock. Who needs an alarm clock when there is something soft and fuzzy jumping on any limb that moves under the blankets at 7:00 a.m.?

Not everyone loves cats. For some, dogs are the way to go, and for others there are other pets. The point is that a pet gives unconditional love, needs your care and devotion and provides comfort and distraction from your pain. They can give you a reason to get out of bed and start a day that just might turn out well. They have done that for me; first Patti O'Kat, then Smudge and Star Cats. They are indeed "angels with fur."

Fur Persons

They are called cats, but that will never do;
Not for my famous feline few.
They are my furry babies dear,
Who rule my house and bring me cheer.

My Patti O'Kat broke me in, set the tone;
When she entered my life, I was never alone.
She was confidant, snuggler, and sometimes demanding,
But, she was always there for me, up on the landing.

She was strict about bedtime and dinnertime too,
But, rewarded with snuggles and purrs, I came through.
She grew old, for a cat, and in time had to go.
I vowed there would be no more sweet calico.

I did not want more cats, I was going to travel,
Be free as a bird; I would tear up the gravel.
So right! And that worked 'till I met Smudge and Star;
They moved in, took over and that's where we are.

Christmas morning

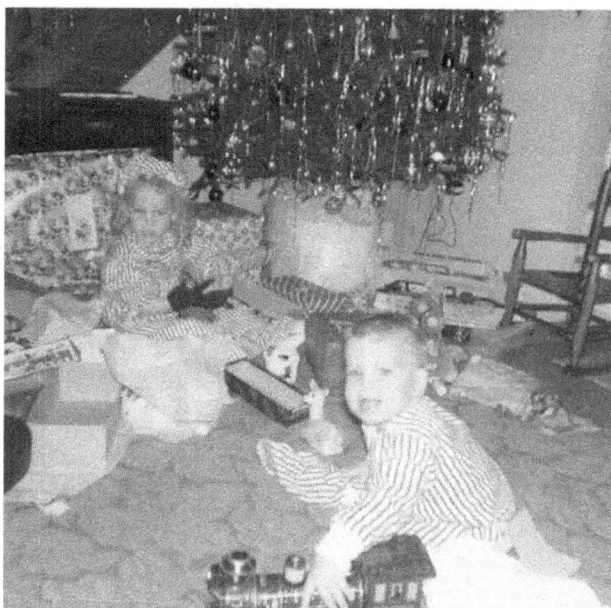

Hallmark & Rockwell
Christmas 2005

Christmas music is everywhere I turn. Happy Holidays!!! It's a time for family, a time for parties and shopping and a jolly good time should be had by all!

Bah and Humbug!! I'm with Scrooge.

Has anyone ever taken a survey to determine how many people really are "Happy Holidaying?" I think not and doubt it would be a worthwhile effort anyway. Who would dare to admit that the Holidays were not likely to be happy? What kind of weirdo would not be happy at the Holiday Season?

I can name a few potential Scrooges. How about a mother who lost her only child last year and has no other children, nor will she ever? How about a child who lost his or her most beloved parent last year, who misses the affection and the guidance and the fun? How about a wife who lost the love of her life last year or the year before, or many years before? How about the children who won't believe in Santa because they don't get any presents? How about the parents of those children, who see the disappointment in those little eyes? How about the old and infirm, who have no family left and live alone and forgotten? I could go on; you know I could. But the reader knows about street people and people without enough to eat, let alone the luxury of toys for the children.

What is the percentage of people who fall into the

108

above categories versus the people with lots of money to spend and family to spend it on and with? Does that really matter? Maybe not, but when Christmas carols are like salt being rubbed into the wounds of people already in pain, it does beg the question, "is that what Christmas is about?"

What is Christmas about? Theoretically, it is a Christian holiday in celebration of the birth of Jesus Christ. We don't know when he was born, but it seemed a good idea to the leaders of the early church to make it December 25, because the Pagans were already celebrating the Winter Solstice at that time. Why not try to turn that Pagan celebration into Christmas? Why not indeed? But is it just possible that it worked the other way around; that the celebration of Jesus' birth turned into a Pagan festival?

Let's think about what we see on TV about the Celebration of Christmas. It's all about finding the best presents for the perfect families that live in every home in America. It's all about finding the perfect dress, getting your makeup right, being thin and young and going to gala parties held in elegant surroundings with exciting, expensively dressed people. Christmas morning, of course, is a family scene with a huge tree in a beautiful room, several adorable children who are beautifully turned out in matching pajamas and a puppy or kitten to frolic with as Mom and Dad beam down on them in pride and delight. This will be followed by the elegant dinner in a formal dining room with grandparents, aunts and uncles in attendance.

Some of these admirable families will be seen attending services on Christmas Eve after the party, before the party or between parties and some will be seen on the Sunday before or after December 25. There are a few services on Christmas Day and some will be seen attending them – some. So, is this a Christian celebration or does it seem just a tiny bit Pagan? I am not casting aspersions on the Pagans, but let's call a spade a spade.

Norman Rockwell, the great American painter, probably had the best of intentions with his paintings of the American people and families. But who lives like that now? Still, this is the image painted on our subconscious brains of how it "should" be, regardless of the fact that very few of us, comparatively, do live such ideal lives. Where Rockwell left off, Hallmark picked up. If any one of the unfortunates who don't have it all, who may be grieving the loss of a loved one, a divorce, poor health, career reverses, old age, etc. need to have a good cry, I recommend watching a Hallmark ad; any of them will do, but some may be a better fit for your pain than others. For example, I lost my only son last year, so the one that goes, "No matter how old your son gets, or how big and strong he gets, a boy will always listen to his mother." (Paraphrased) The scene, the background, the way the words are spoken – it's all pure genius. I burst into tears whenever I hear it and I expect that I am not the only one for whom Hallmark ads evoke that jolly response. Of course, it is running throughout the holidays; just perfect for the first year in 41 that he won't be hugging me and wishing me "Merry Christmas, Mom."

No, I am not an unbiased reporter, but I have had 25 years to really think this through. My only daughter died in 1980, so the Holidays lost their glow for me and I must wonder how many others feel as I do and put on their "happy face" to the world, hoping that nobody will see through the mask. I remember how shocked I was when my grandmother said to me, many years ago, that she was always glad when Christmas was over. When I asked her why, she said that I would learn as I grew older and she was right. She was elderly and living with one of her children and his family. She had lost one of her other adult children some years prior to our conversation and her health was uncertain. She could not afford to give gifts, as she was financially dependent on her children; all of which made the Holiday Season a very difficult time for her.

I understand that all of this is part of the American culture and I don't mean to imply that joy and fun should be set aside for those of us who are not feeling joyful or having much fun. I have had some wonderful holidays and years; I don't mean to complain, although I guess that is exactly what I am doing. My hope is that some sensitivity might be shown to those of us who cannot share the jolly spirit, as a result of our own life experience. There are so many people out there helping others in need, feeding them, clothing them, etc. This country is full of the very best kind of people in the world and they should be as happy as they can be. But, what's wrong with Classical music in the shops instead of carols that bring back memories now painful to recall? Why must 90% of the TV programming be about the perfect holiday for the perfect people? Why can't Hallmark sell cards without being so maudlin that they bring people to tears? Why can't life go on as at any other time of the year? That would not stop the revelers from reveling.

OK, I'm off my soapbox and I feel better for getting this off my chest even if nobody every reads it or if, in reading, disagrees. I'll find ways to cope, as I have done before, and I will find some happiness and joy in my life. But, I will always maintain that Rockwell and Hallmark have much for which to answer.

Christmas

Me and mine and many more
Don't want to go into that store.
Don't want to hear the carol sing,
Don't want to hear the glad bells ring.

The bells and carols hurt our ears
And bring us all the way to tears.
The bells are not glad bells to us;
We really need to skip the fuss.

When hearts are broken, loved ones gone;
When it is hard to face a dawn,
How do we deal with all that glee?
With Holidays that they won't see?

Play Beethoven, Liszt or Bach.
Go ahead and play that rock!
Anything but carols, please,
Give our hearts a little ease.

When life is full of joy and love,
The sound of bells from up above
Delights your heart and fills your ears
With joy; you never think of tears.

We're glad for you, please understand
We've been there too and it was grand.
But, it won't dim your joy of Yule
To skip the bells and carols cruel.

Enjoy them in some other places,
Only not in public spaces.
Good will toward men and women too.
This would help and we'd thank you.

Imagine My Surprise

It was 1984 and I had just returned from a period of living and working in Georgia. Until I could find a home of my own, I was sharing a house with a friend who recently separated from her husband. My return to New Jersey had been the first week of January and my birthday was the third week of January, a date I was anticipating with dread. I had gone directly to work, as my job had transferred me, so there had not been time to reconnect with old friends, and I had doubts if my son would even remember the date. He was working and sharing a house with some friends and he had a very active social life. I decided that my best course of action was to ignore the day anyway. I was depressed. I missed Evie; Albert was very independent and a relationship that I desperately wanted to work had failed.

Of course, my birthday fell on a weekend in a year when I had no plans! I decided to do the laundry, errands, shopping and treat it like any other weekend. It was cold and snowy and I did not know if the friend I was living with would make it home for dinner, so I planned to "wing it" and go to bed early with Patti O'Kat and a good book. I was feeling pretty sorry for myself when somebody knocked on the door.

It was Albert with his current girlfriend, a big hug for me and a brightly wrapped package. They had not eaten, so I ordered pizza delivered and we had a great time together.

He did not have much spending money in those days, as he was training for retail management, but he bought me a "Greatest Mom" mug that I cherish to this day, along with the memory of that night. Later in the evening my friend came home and brought a birthday cake with candles and ice cream, so we had a wonderful little party. Young people are not always mindful of what their parents need, but my Albert never failed to come through for me when I really needed him; he always seemed to know. That dreaded day turned out to be a fine day and one I'll always remember with a smile and a grateful heart.

Albert was living about thirty miles from where I was now located, both of us to be near our jobs. As it happened, he met a girl who lived near me and I began to see much more of him. He would pop in on Friday night and let me know that he would be staying the weekend with us; then he would go pick up the new girl and I would get to fix him breakfast and hear what was going on in his life. Things were definitely looking up.

My friend and her husband decided to divorce, so by spring the house was on the market and quickly sold, leaving us looking for accommodations. Albert was spending more and more time with me, so I asked him if he would like to move into my new apartment with me. He declined on two counts: 1) his job and 2) he was "too old to live with his mother." I accepted that, but got a two bedroom apartment anyway for his weekend visits. Within a month of my move into my own apartment, he had joined me. He had been accepted by the union to which his father belonged and could easily work from my area. This was a great time for both of us. I was SO glad to have him with me and I spoiled him as much as possible. He had been through so much when he was so young and I wanted to make up to him some of what he had lost.

During the year in the apartment, I was actively looking for a condo to purchase and I found one that I liked. We had the same conversation and I got the same answer from him minus the job reason: "I'm too old to be living at home." So, I bought a two bedroom condo and he moved in three months after I did. Again, I was a very happy Mom. I had my 6'7" baby back home for a while. He moved out when he married and he never came back to stay afterwards. The second bedroom was used as a library and guest room and most of the guests were my grandchildren. That was good too.

Furniture

The chair and the sideboard stand together still,
So many years later, so far from the hill
That first felt my footsteps and first saw my face,
As it stood there eternal, majestic with grace.

That chair held Grandmother, when she rocked me to sleep,
And the sideboard's old mirror would give me a peep
At both our reflections, and I felt it kept one
Of my Great Grandmother with her daughter and son.

They stand in a room they now share with TV,
The mirror reflection again is of three;
Me rocking grandchildren, like Grandmom rocked me
In the old Mission Rocker, part of my family tree.

If it's true that reflections stay on in a mirror,
That old sideboard mirror is full as can be.
It must hold Great Grandmother, Grandmom and Mother,
Along with my children, grandchildren and me.

As I rock my grandchildren, like Grandmom rocked me
In the old Mission Rocker close to the TV,
I know life has changed, but not the best part,
Which is keeping these grandchildren close to my heart.

Why?

Six days after my sixty-sixth birthday at about six in the morning, my phone rang. The room was completely dark; my birthday is in January. I knew why it was ringing before I picked it up, but I did not want to hear it. As I moved to pick up the receiver, both cats jumped off the bed in consternation. We don't get phone calls at six in the morning.

It was my daughter-in-law and she was distraught. "You need to call Judy and come down here as fast as possible. But call Judy. Don't come down by yourself." In answer to my question, "What's wrong?" she repeated what she had said first, but her voice was shaking more with the repetition. I repeated my question more loudly and she responded in kind, "Albert's dead. You've got to get down here as fast as you can, but don't come alone. Get Judy." I asked her to repeat it, because I wanted to be sure. She did, but she was breaking down. I said that I would be there as soon as possible and put the phone back on the hook.

Albert had been fine when I spoke to him the day before. I got up, went downstairs, fed the cats, got something to eat and drank a mug of coffee. Then, I showered, dressed and bundled up for the 32 mile drive. I did not call Judy and I could not hurry. I could only do one thing at a time and I was on auto pilot.

I drove as fast as road conditions would permit; they

were not the best or the worst. There was lots of snow, but the main roads had been cleared. I had a strong sense of deja vu, but this time I was all alone in the car.

When I approached their house, the street was lined with cars and people were coming out, but I could not tell who they were at first. As they drew closer, I saw my step grandson and two of my former daughter-in-law's sisters approaching. When they realized it was me, someone took my arm on each side and they walked me down the slippery driveway and into the house, offering sympathy as best they could; both were in tears. We were all in shock. They told me that the ambulance had just taken him away.

Walking into the warm house, I was greeted by two of my daughters-in-law; his current wife and her predecessor, and my grandson. I found out soon enough that he had discovered his father unresponsive, called his stepmother and then 911. It was all surreal to all of us. When I heard the whole story, I was glad that I had been unable to move any faster, because I would have seen something I could not have borne.

When his son found him, he was only partially dressed, as he had left his bed to sleep on the sofa. He had been in pain, which made him restless, and when he realized that his movements were keeping his wife awake, he got up and went downstairs. That is how he was found and the EMTs laid him on the hardwood floor to try and bring him back; my dignified son, so proud of his appearance and so meticulous about his clothing. I know that he would not have wanted me to see him that way and am glad that I did not. It was hard enough for the others who loved him to witness what happened.

As I write this, it has been one year and two months from that day and every one has been a struggle. I have comforted myself in the time-honored fashion, always used before in times of trouble. When the going gets tough, I eat, and in the last 20 years, I have been washing it down with red wine. The result is that I weigh twenty pounds more than I did on January 28, 2005. Heaven knows what I would weigh if I was not making fairly routine visits to the local health club to lift weights and walk. The doctors have told me that I need to do this, because I have osteopenia and osteoarthritus. While it is helping me to maintain flexibility and build bone, it helps control weight and it helps to control mood. Some of my friends have joined me over the course of the year and I am not sure if they are doing it for themselves or for me, but it is good for them too, so I encourage them to continue. They can't always be there, so I go alone sometimes and that is more difficult; not the weights part, but the walking part. Albert had downloaded CDs of some of my favorite songs (and some of his) for me to listen to while I walked and I find them hard to use now. So I use other CDs and try not to think about him as I walk. I did not think it would be the thing to do to walk the track with tears streaming down my face.

§

Yesterday, I got in a twenty minute walk in the park, which was bonus exercise on a day when I don't go to the health club. I did some errands and came home to pack up some things for Goodwill in the basement. This is one of the things I have to keep working at: cleaning out my life's clutter. I have always been, like many people, a "holiday" person and in the pursuit of more fun holidays I have collected so much STUFF.

I won't be using much of that from now on, because I don't have a family. It is family stuff with memories of holiday visits from my son with his family, and some of the stuff arrived with them as gifts. So, I pack away the wooden letters spelling Happy Easter, because those Easters are over, and I pack away some decorative rabbits and eggs.

Some things I must keep, like the little basket that I gave him on one happy Easter many years ago with a gold (vermeil) bracelet in it. My niece was getting married in another state and we went to the wedding together. It was Easter weekend, and I secreted away the basket, the bracelet, and the peanut butter egg that "the bunny" brought for him every Easter every since he was big enough to eat candy. On Easter morning, I brought it out of its hiding place in my luggage and gave it to him. We had a great time that weekend. It is one of many lovely memories I shared with my boy.

§

But back to yesterday. I had collected decorations for every holiday in the year, so the boxes for Goodwill contained Christmas, Halloween, Valentine's Day, etc., etc., etc. I hope they add fun to the families' holidays who take them home from the Goodwill shop. My own "holidays" will be much plainer from now on. Oh, I will still put out some very special things, like my mother's Easter eggs in the original basket, and I hope that some family member will want them when I am gone, but only a few, very special things will I keep.

It is hard to imagine future holidays at all. I got through this first year without him with the loving support of extended family members and friends. When my birthday rolled around again, my grandson made it a point to spend part of it with me. He really wanted to be with me on that day and I don't think I will ever be able to impress upon him how much that meant to me.

This year, I need to establish the New Normal for holidays and I still don't know how I will do that. My first instinct is to ignore them completely, spend the days alone and avoid TV. I have done that on certain occasions in the past and it sort of worked. I am not sure if that is what I want to do. Maybe I could volunteer somewhere and make a better holiday for someone else, but where? I can't do anything that requires me to stand for a long period of time. Easter is coming at me and, worse yet, Mother's Day.

But, I digress.......

After I finished working at the computer last night, when it was my "wind down" time, I sat staring at a wall and trying to decide whether last night would be the first night without binging on food and wine before going to bed. Actually, it would not be the first night; it would be the first night in about a week. Sometimes I have gotten myself motivated, planned a light snack, and stuck with the plan for a few days. Then, something would happen to upset me and the pain would come to consume me again. The food and wine would be taken for those medicinal purposes and I would struggle along until I felt strong enough and good enough to try and break that bad habit again. I thought that last night might be the night, but I was wrong. I started reading with just a small glass of wine, but then I decided a little snack would not hurt that much and in no time at all the promise to myself was broken again.

I did sleep very well, straight through the night, and woke up feeling good. The sun was shining and I was thinking about what is left of my life. I never planned to have Albert take care of me in my old age. I have long-term care insurance that I can ill afford, which I purchased to ensure that I would never be a burden to him, and now I am sure that I won't. That said, in the back of my mind, there was the security of knowing that he loved me and would never let me be in need. That security is gone and looking ahead at the age of 67 can be a frightening aspect indeed.

The cats must be fed and I love them dearly. They have been a great comfort to me during this time with their constant and unconditional love and I don't want to let them down. They are truly the only creatures in the world who depend on me daily, who watch for me to come home and who would miss me in a big way if I were not here. I worry about their futures too.

I watch them eat and calculate their probable life

span and mine; suddenly, I have an idea. What I need is a ten year plan. Star Cat is 10 and Smudge Cat is almost 8. Both of them have had some health problems, so I am thinking that I will probably lose both of them within the next ten years. Furthermore, I doubt that I will live longer than ten more years. My father lived to be almost 80, but my mother died at 70, my sister at 75 and my brother at 61. I don't need to worry about what will happen to me when I am truly old and doddering; I probably won't get there and that cheers me up immensely. I can look forward ten years without feeling so frightened and insecure. My savings might actually get me to that point! And if I take care of myself during those ten years, I can take care of my little buddies as long as they need me.

My role in life seems to be taking care of people who die and leave me. It is like the game we played in school "The Farmer in the Dell." At the end of the game, "The Cheese Stands Alone." That is what I feel like: the cheese. It is not surprising that my parents, aunts and uncles are dead; they would all be over 100 years old by now. What does me down is the loss of my children, my siblings and some of my cousins and friends. Naturally, we have all moved around the country and most of those still living are not close enough to be the shoulder needed for crying.

So, how do I learn to live well under these circumstances, because I am alive and might as well make the best of it if I am going to continue? The health club is a start and I need to keep working at that. The biggest change I need to make, physically, is that bedtime snack. I need to find and become involved with a local church, to have a church family. I think that is the next most critical piece. Do I need a part time job? Maybe. I have to take charge of what is left of my life and it is hard to start over at 67.

§

Have you ever had a dream that was so real that the sounds in it woke you up? I did when I was married and my children were young. In the dream, I was standing on a second story porch, the kind that runs around the second level of a house and has stairs that go down to the ground. The house was made of wood and there was a door and windows behind where I stood. I was wearing a long gown of some kind, maybe a nightgown, and had long brown hair. I was holding a baby boy in Doctor Denton pajamas in my arms. Behind me, the house was burning and I could hear glass breaking. I was thinking that the glass was in the picture frames in the room behind me and that I was losing the pictures of my wedding and family. I could not get out through the house, because the fire was too far advanced and I could not go down the outside staircase, because that was burning too. The flames were coming up through the stairs and I had to decide whether the baby stood a better chance if I threw him down into some bushes or if I jumped with him. There was another loud sound of breaking glass and that woke me.

My husband was sleeping soundly beside me and there was no light or heat in the room that would have indicated fire. I checked on each of the children and they were both sleeping peacefully in their bedrooms. Even the dogs and cats were asleep and wondered what I was doing roaming around at that hour. There was clearly nothing wrong, so I went back to bed, and eventually, back to sleep.

You may well ask what this has to do with anything on my mind today or why I remember it at all. I will answer the first question, and that will answer the second, but first I have something else to share with you.

I did a past life regression last year. It started in a class I took on Psychic Development and I finished it later at home on the swing on my back deck. I went back to a life when I had been a farmer's wife. I think it was in the 17th or early 18th century by the way we were dressed. In the early part of the regression, my husband was clearing out trees and building a house, barn and outbuildings. I was very happy and we were going to have a baby. It was unsettling when I did this in class under a "mass hypnosis" kind of atmosphere, because it was new and everything was so clear to me. I waited some weeks before trying it on my own. The class was over now and no more was required of me, but I wanted to see a later period in that life. I had the information from the class and a book that gave instruction on how to do that and I felt I had to try. I went back to the same clearing, but it was much bigger and there were more buildings and farm animals. There were also children and I was working hard and loving every minute of it. I had a very happy marriage, something which I did not attain in this life, and I loved being a mother. That was enough for that time, so

I returned to my own life happy to know that I could do self-hypnosis and that I could regress and return myself. A week or two later, I decided to look further into the future of that life. This time, I found myself very sick and distraught about what would happen to my family when I died, because I knew I would die. There were six or seven children, all quite young, and my husband had little or no help on the farm, which seemed to be isolated. I could not imagine what would happen to all of them when I was gone.

I brought myself back and out of it and then I thought about what it meant to this life. There is a school of thought with the premise that we are reincarnated into each life in order to learn certain lessons that bring us closer to God. This makes sense to me and I approached the two experiences described above from that perspective. The dream had haunted me for some forty years and the regression was a new experience; they were equally real to me.

In both the dream and the regression, my primary fear was for my children. I wanted to save them and I did not want to leave them. In this life, I saw both of my children from birth to death. I was there for them when they needed me; at least to the extent I could be. I never had to face death and wondering what would happen to them or worrying about how much they would miss me. It was me who would be left alone to miss them. I found this thought curiously comforting, because it offered an explanation for something that had been completely a mystery to me.

Why would God take away both of my children and leave me alone in my old age? I am not a perfect person, I have made and continue to make mistakes, but that is a terrible punishment and I am not a bad person. Then again, I believe in a loving God and in his Grace. I had prayed and prayed for my children, and in times of trouble, had sent donations to Christian organizations asking for prayer for them, but my prayers were not answered as I expected them to be answered. If this life was ordained for me before my birth, it explains in a satisfactory manner why my prayers seem to have been ignored. They were not, but God sees the whole picture and the wisdom of man or woman is not that good.

Some people will say that this is "woo woo" stuff and they have the right to their own beliefs. I only know what I know and that is what I have shared.

The Voice Inside

Can I trust just what I feel?
It seems farfetched and can't be real
I tell myself; and yet, I know
The voice inside is how I grow.

There's more to us than mind and form
Although some say that is the norm.
Our body works all on its own,
Our minds can think and plan alone.

Bodies feel pain but minds don't feel;
They plan and execute and deal.
There's something more we cannot see
Or touch but it IS you and me.

The voice inside, the soul, the guide,
The spirit, knows nothing of pride.
It's there for all who let it be
For guidance and serenity.

Not everyone will hear that voice,
To listen is each person's choice.
Prayer is the way to seek this source
Followed by silence and sometimes remorse.

Grief

There is really nothing that I can say about the grief process that has not been said before now, so that is not what this is about. I think that we all experience grief from an individual perspective, because we are all individuals. That is not to say that we don't all go through the same stages, but we don't experience them all the same way. For example, some people linger in the anger stage, whereas others linger in the regret stage and the time for those stages, as well as the order in which they occur, will differ by individual.

I found myself bouncing around them quite unpredictably and without warning. Sometimes, I thought I was Bipolar because of the speed of my mood swings, especially in the beginning.

Some months after Evie's death and after I had returned to work, I was walking down the street heading home on a late spring day. It had been a good day at work and the weather was beautiful. Flowers were blooming, the sun was warm and it felt good to walk after being cooped up in an office all day. It was one of those days that make you feel good all over; and I did, until I saw a pogo stick leaning against a porch post. The memories flooded back and it was as if I lost her yesterday.

I remembered, in vivid detail, the year that she really wanted a pogo stick for Christmas, and so Santa brought her one. She was a danger to man, beast and especially herself on that pogo, but she had so much fun with it. When the weather turned warm in the spring, she would hop it out the front door, down the porch steps, across the driveway and down the street, grinning all the way. The skinned knees made no difference to Evie; she was getting good at it.

Just glancing at that stick leaning on the porch post brought me to my knees. I cried all the way home and kept right on crying when I got there.

There was a period of time after she died that I dreaded hearing music in public, because so many songs reminded me of her and the tears would start. Music was a connection between us and got pulled into our conversations so often. There is something about music that reaches a part of your soul that is not easily accessible any other way. Have you ever tried to avoid public music? I had always been able to control my emotions, a skill I learned early in my life; but, that skill was not working too well and music is piped in so many places: the grocery store, the mall, most restaurants. I got in and out as quickly as possible until I got past that stage of my grief.

And there was my night job with the trio to consider. We had to delete some songs from my list, because there were songs I could not get through any more. Evie had particularly liked the way I sang "Seventeen," which I took great pride in because neither of them were inclined to applaud my style. They thought that songs should be sung the way they were performed by the people who made them hits, but I did my own interpretations. That worked for the members of my group and for the people who came to hear us, but not always for Evie and Albert. Anyway, "Seventeen" was off the playlist along with some others.

Another trigger was scent. Evie was fond of musk and that was her personal scent of choice. I could not bear to part with the last handbag she used, because it was fabric and held the scent for a long time; I could pick it up, inhale and remember. It was many years later that I disposed of it and of the remainder of her clothing. There was comfort for me in knowing it was there. I knew that one of the "laws" of moving through grief is to get rid of the loved one's personal effects, but those laws don't work for everybody.

I still have some of her things and I know that I need to reduce the number of her things that I keep as I continue with my un-cluttering project. The clothing is gone and there really is not much left, but there are things she made when she was doing ceramics, some of her candles, a small wall hanging, the handprint in clay that she made in Kindergarten, things like that. I finally parted with her Weeble-Wobble. Every time I looked at it, I could see her balancing on it, falling off it and laughing the whole time. Even though she was eighteen years old, she had carried that with her. I kept her jewelry boxes and some of her jewelry; two of her necklaces are hanging from the mirror in my car with my crystals. She did not have much of value because we had little to spare for jewelry.

I searched, asked questions and made all efforts to

find the silver guitar charm which she wore as a necklace but I never found it. She had lent it to my fiancé to wear for a month, then she took it back and I think she may have loaned it to someone else for the same purpose. It was her way of showing trust and affection and it was very special to her. I thought she would want to wear it forever, but I could not find it and so she could not wear it when we buried her.

One thing I have learned is that your life can totally change in an instant and there will come a day when this house must be emptied, whether it is because I have decided to move, because I need to enter some facility for care or because I have joined my children. At the same time, I see no reason to get rid of things that I continue to use and enjoy; I am still living and enjoying in spite of my losses. It is the items that I don't use and can live without, items that would mean nothing to anybody else, that need to go. If Albert had lived, he would have known about everything in my home and he would have made the right decisions for disposition of my things in my absence, but he did not and I need to make some decisions now while I can.

When I lost Albert, I had very few of his things in my home, because he did not live with me in the house I now occupy, but his widow told me to ask for anything that I wanted and what I wanted most was the fleece he always wrapped me in when I got cold at his house. She lovingly gave it to me, and on those tough, cold days, I wear it all day. Let the experts say what they will; it comforts me.

He left some things in my home when he moved the

last time, among which is his teen-age desk. I use that for a TV stand and extra storage in the dining room, because he never found a place for it in his new home. It is not a piece of furniture that I would have chosen, but he picked it out himself for his bedroom when we moved during his high school years and he really liked it a lot. I like looking at it and remembering him doing his homework there. Of course, I have the many gifts he brought to me over the years. He was always generous and sensitive to my interests and tastes, so he always knew exactly what would delight me. It is hard to name a favorite, but the box that contained the gold heart set with diamonds that he gave me one Valentine's Day would certainly top the list. The box is heart-shaped and covered with red silk and it contained a chip, so every time I open it he says, "Happy Valentine's Day, Mom. I love you."

For some people, a complete change of scene is the way to move into a new life, but I know that the old life and memories will be with me anyway, and it is comforting to me to look at a spot in my home or an object where I have a happy memory of him. It seems to me that this keeps his spirit close and I know that the spirits of Evie and Albert are telling me to get on with my life. They don't hold me back, but they don't want me to forget them; as if I would choose to or would be able to forget them!

In the last few years before he died, Albert surprised me with gifts of framed photographs of him and his sister as children and one of him and me that I cherish. I told him then and still believe that it is the best picture of us together that I have seen. One of the things that I like about it is that I can see a resemblance to me in that photo that is not always apparent. I think he knew that and I think that is why he had that picture enlarged for me. His looks were really a composite of his father and me, but his father's features were dominant. With Evie, it was the same, but in spite of having her father's blond hair and blue eyes, she looked more like me. They both got the best of each parent, in my opinion.

Unlike some bereaved parents, it also comforts me to take care of the cemetery. I will admit that it is easier when there is someone to help me with it, but I often do it alone and feel a sense of comfort knowing that their graves look loved. They now lie side by side for eternity and I have made my arrangements with the funeral home and had my stone set at the foot of Evie's grave. My ashes will be interred between them. I chose to put my stone at the foot of her grave, because she was never married and never had children. Albert leaves family behind and the spot at the foot of his grave should be saved for that reason.

Because I believe that I have made it plain that I believe in the life of the spirit, you may be surprised that being buried by my children should mean so much to me, but it does. I want my physical remains with theirs for eternity too. Again, it comforts me to know that I will share that shady space in the country cemetery with them when my time comes.

My choices would not be right for all, but they are for me. My grieving is not over, nor do I think I will ever stop missing my children, but I am still Mignon and I will make the most of the rest of my life that I can; I know that is what they would want for me and that is what I want too.

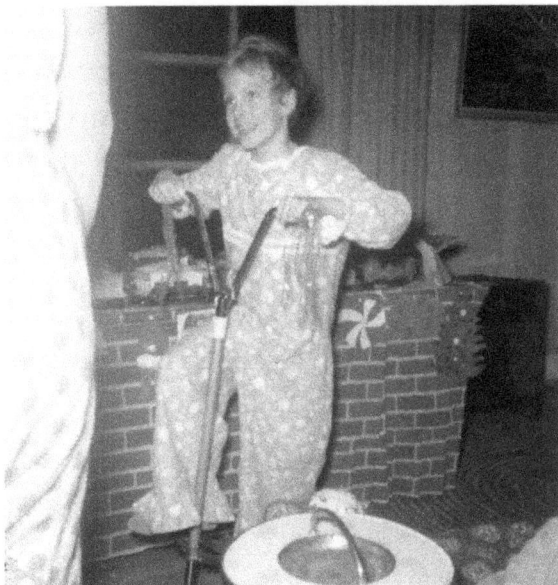

Evie on the pogo stick

NOTE: Evie wrote this shortly before she played her guitar and sang with a friend at the Baccalaureate Service held for graduation at her high school in her junior year. I don't know which of her friends she wrote this poem for; she had many friends. She and I shared the problem of stage fright in spite of the fact that we both loved to perform. Evie did a terrific job that night! She would probably have played for her own senior graduation ceremonies, too, if she had lived.

Debut
1979 by EvieG

I'm standing on the stage,
Just seeing empty chairs.
Thinking of the future
And about 1,000 stares.

I'm not afraid of dumb mistakes;
Just terrified of crowds.
I can't pretend they're just not there,
Or hide by playing loud.

Soon it'll all be over.
I'll be done with my debut,
But until then, I think I'll need
Support from friends like you.

I think I'll try to find a face
Of a friend to hold on tight,
And I know that if you are that face,
Everything will turn out right.

So, now I'm going to ask
A favor of a friend.
Just be there when I'm on that stage,
And smile at the end?

My Favorite Room

With trees for one wall,
The sky for a ceiling,
And with birdsongs for music,
Pure joy is my feeling.

My deck's full of flowers,
The birds fill the trees,
The Roses of Sharon,
Curtsey in the breeze.

This place full of beauty,
Of vision and sound,
Is blessing me daily;
I feel it surround.

The God of my being
Did find it for me,
And surely I'm grateful
Today just to be.

The Dream

Sometimes, when I am half awake, I think I hear the humming of the pool filter in the back yard and I feel such contentment. Then I open my eyes, realize that I am alone and recognize that the humming comes from another unit's air conditioner. And I wish I had not waked up.

In my dream with the pool filter sound track, I was lying next to my husband with my children sleeping soundly down the hall. I could look forward to a summer day of watching children in the pool, playing with the dogs and cats, running, laughing and (yes) fighting. I did not take it for granted, even then, and it was not always the paradise I seem to be describing. So, what was it? It was the life I had always imagined would be mine and I loved it. I have not lived that life for many years.

It seems to me now that I have lived several lives in this one. In fact, I created a collage of photographs from different times in my life in order to see them together and try to see some kind of coherence. The segments of my life are so different that they might just as well be considered different lives, except that some threads hold them together. They are strong threads to have held these people and parts of my past in my life through all the changes; yet, they are fragile and they can break. I feel that, without them, I may float away into nothingness, totally disconnected from everything that matters to me.

Sometimes, I think that I already live among the spirits as much as I live among the living. Why wouldn't I when I have lost more of the people that I have loved than I have kept in my life. Sometimes I feel a presence so strongly that I seem to see a movement out of the corner of my eye. Spirits can't hold me or tell me that everything will be all right, but I can feel their love and caring and it helps.

So do the memories that warm the fragments of my heart. But, there are other memories that still chill me to the bone.

§

"Mommy, what happens when you die?" That was not the question I expected from my three year old daughter, so I had not prepared a response. It was 1964 and she already had a baby brother, so I had been ready to deal with the "How do babies get there?" question for some time, but she never brought it up. Her question about dying stopped me in my tracks and I stood looking across the unmade bed at her sweet little face. It was a warm spring day and I had opened the front windows in the bedroom, which was on the second floor of our row house. Of course, there were screens in the windows, but when she started leaning on the sill to look out, I told her to come back and sit in the chair. I explained further, "If you were to lean on the window screen or lose your balance and fall against it, the screen could fall out and you might fall with it. You would be sure to get hurt and could even die from a fall like that, so you must never get so close to the window."

I guess her question was natural, given my caution to her, and she was a very bright three year old; still, I was taken aback by the seriousness of her question and a shadow fell across my heart that had never been there before. This was not to be the last time that shadow came to visit.

I remember being in the hospital on New Year's Eve 1961 when she arrived, two weeks late, and so beautiful and perfect. She had some blond down on her little head and big blue eyes that kept their color. She did not have red, wrinkled skin; it was creamy and everything about her was just lovely. She was our first child and the only grandchild to whom my in-laws had access. My parents had other grandchildren, but I was the baby of my family and she was my first child. She was adored by all.

Her dad was home on leave from military service and had only six weeks left to serve, but we did not know how long then, as he was extended for the "Bay of Pigs" crisis. At birth she looked so much like him. She grew to look more like me, but with his complexion, curly blond hair and long, long legs. She grew into a beautiful woman, who had her own look, ideas and personality. She also had more talent than either of us or both combined; talent as a musician and as an artist. Oh yes, she was also a poet and all by age eighteen.

She went through a very difficult period as she came into her teens and one of the areas of disagreement was her eighth grade graduation. She was not going! She was the tallest girl in the class and very self conscious and *She*

Was Not Going to walk down that aisle and up on that stage for people to stare at her. I bought her the dress of her choice and had it altered to fit perfectly. We found the perfect shoes to match it, but *She Still Was Not Going.*

She did go, very reluctantly, and I have pictures that will never let me forget a moment of that day. She looked beautiful, but she did not believe it for a minute.

"NO, I want THIS dress!" I recall when her first day of school was coming up in the next week or two and we were shopping with her Pop Pop, who wanted to buy her a new dress. She looked so cute in the little sailor dress with the wide collar, but my five-year-old wasn't in a Navy kind of mood. She had picked up a straight lined little red dress with a print of small yellow flowers and she thought it was just perfect for her first day of school. Her step-grandfather had taken us shopping and was becoming more uncomfortable by the moment. He had inherited three stepsons as teenagers when he married my mother-in-law, and had no clue about little girls (or much about big ones), but he had a solution, and we walked out with both dresses.

I guess I don't have to mention which dress was worn on the first day. I have a photo of her standing by the roadside waiting for the bus in her little red dress with her lunchbox in her hand. She can hardly contain her excitement.

About Dreams

What happens when we dream at night?
Do our spirits take to flight?
What strange scenes we may come upon
Between the darkness and the dawn.

What can they mean; how do we know
Why we would picture things just so?
I dream a big house with many a room
And winding halls, all dark and gloom.

But, other nights, I dream sweet things
Of happy days and kids on swings;
Of splashing water and childish glee
And cookies with a glass of tea.

I never want those dreams to end!
Let them continue while I spend
The rest of my life in this happy dream state;
I won't get up at all, let alone get up late.

Evie's first day of first grade

Two Years

Sometimes, life changes come on gradually and you can see them coming from afar. Sometimes, like tsunamis, you wake up abruptly one morning to find your world broken into shattered shards with the most vital pieces missing forever.

On January 28, 2005, the phone rang, the words, "He's dead," the drive through the snow, alone in an unreal world, to a place I never wanted to go. The destination was the rest of my life, now empty of meaning and most of the love; a lonely place, a frightening place, my forever after place.

For a while, friends and relatives appear, offer what comfort they can, try to understand and keep in touch. But how can they understand? None of them has had their entire family wiped out; none of them is facing old age and death alone. Still, they try and it helps.

Then, there is the alternation between denial, despair and that fragile sliver of hope. It is an emotional roller coaster ride of high denial, bottoming out despair and tenuous, uncertain hope. I think of the words of an old (like me) song: "What can I hope for? I wish I knew."

I read self-help books, I watch Dr. Phil and Oprah, I see a therapist, I pray, I meditate and I cry (thanks to the therapist). I had learned to automatically suppress my tears when I lost my daughter; now that I have lost my son too, I must cry or I will die. Then I ask myself, what would be so bad about dying? It looks pretty inviting from here, but from somewhere deep inside, I know there is some reason why I am surviving both of my children. There has to be some purpose to my life beyond being a parent. I am a grandparent, but they are teens and have no need of me; that can't be the reason. I continue to search.

But, while I am searching, life is moving on, more changes are taking place and I have no choice but to accommodate to them. My closest relationship since losing my boy has been his widow. We were close when he lived and became even closer when we lost him. We clung together and somehow held each other up, at least some of the time. We got through the worst of it (so far) together.

Now, she is trying to tell me, gently, kindly, and carefully, that she is going to sell the house and move far away to start a new life. She needs to do this and I understand. She owes me nothing. She has been nothing but good to me and was nothing but good to my son as long as I have known her. I want her to be happy again and I need to bless her and send her on her way, but I have not been able to say the right words yet. I have told her that she needs to do what she needs to do and I have told her, without any acrimony, that I will miss her, but I have not told her that I know she needs to go, that she needs to start a new life and that I want her to do that.

Because I don't! When she sells their house and goes away, I lose more of my son. We share memories of him and I will not be able to walk into the house where I got my last hug from him. I will tend the cemetery alone, again. The best comfort I get there is seeing my own stone waiting for me next to them. This is very selfish of me and I really don't want to hold her back; I just don't know how to endure losing her too.

My life is empty, but that is not her fault. Whether I want to or not, I am living and it is up to me to build a new life, regardless of my age. If I am not going to do that, I might as well fold up and die. Neither of us can live on past memories. We can thank God for what we had and recall good times, but we must live in the present and the fullness or emptiness of our lives is up to each of us. She loves me and feels responsible for me. I need to bless her and set her free.

So, this is what is next. I have applied for a part time job in a library, and I know that there will be lots of applicants and my chances are slim. I don't even know if I can do what they would want me to do, but the important thing is that I have begun to move in a new direction. If this application is rejected, I will look for something else that I would like to do and apply for that until I find a spot that suits. I need the money, I need the stimulation, I need the change, and I need the social contacts.

And I will continue to write, to watch Dr. Phil and Oprah, to see a therapist, to pray, to meditate and to cry. Most important, I will try to remember that none of life's events are under my control. God, Who is in control, sees the "big picture" of which I see only a small part. I must remember to go forward in faith and to listen for the still small voice to direct me in making decisions. I need to remember that He will never abandon me and that He will reunite me with my loved ones when the time is right.

Maybe tomorrow, I will be excited about the opportunities that I may find and the new life that I may build. Tonight, I can only grieve for what I have lost. It seems ungrateful when I have had so much, but it is human to grieve losses and I have had many in my 67 years. God must think I'm very strong to give me this mountain to climb, and He must be right.

I read in my Bible that "Weeping may endure for a night, but joy cometh in the morning." (Psalm 30:5) and I wait for that sunrise.

In Season

I like to stretch out by the sea
And think and plan and dream and be;
To hear the roaring of the surf,
Bigger and stronger than sorrow or mirth.

Perhaps perspective can be found
When close to the sand and sound,
And the strength to face your life,
And, maybe, in season, a reason.

Toasting the future with Albert at his wedding

Staying Connected

It has been so important to me to stay connected after each of my losses; from the losses that were hurtful and saddening to the ones that brought me to my knees. I was not always aware that it was important and there were times when I just wanted to be left alone; times when I needed to be alone. Those times are part of mourning a loss, part of accepting the changes and part of healing, so I don't mean to suggest that I did not need time to myself or that it is a bad thing. It only becomes unhealthy if you don't stay connected. It is one thing to tell family and/or friends that you need some space, some time to rest and absorb your new reality and to take that time for as long as you need it, but I found that getting stuck in that spot led me into a downward spiral. This is so easy to fall into when you live alone, as I do.

When I lost Evie, I was not living alone; I had a job and a busy life. I was "protected" from being by myself by those who loved me and that was done with the best of intentions. I think that they were concerned by my level of depression and feared that I might harm myself; in time, they realized that I would not do that and my life began to move in the direction of that "new normal" that we have to find. It was still busy, but I found some time for myself and began to write in the journals, which is one of my most successful methods for processing feelings and information. Isolation was not an option at that time and the problem I encountered from being constantly in company was that I was holding back my feelings and they were festering. The depression could not lift until I faced them, but who knew that? I did not want to bring down the people around me; I did not want to lose people I loved because I was such a "downer." So I donned my smiley face and when I could not keep it up, I would decide to take a nap or read a book while sipping a glass of wine or I might get into a cleaning frenzy and tire myself out. If I was alone for a while, the tears would flow and release some of the pressure and I would write in my journal.

But when I lost Albert, I was alone with my cats and there were periods of time when I did not want to go out of the house at all for days on end; it suited me admirably if the phone did not ring. Although I would read my email, I did not want to respond. My theory was that nobody would want an answer from me in the mood I was in, so I would put it off for another day.

My concern with the welfare of the cats got out of hand to the point where I did not want to leave them for any extended period of time (e.g. 5 or 6 hours), because one of them might get sick. When one of them did get sick, I went into panic mode. I simply could not face losing one more living thing that I loved; I had no resources left to face another loss.

The thing about getting stuck in a place like this is that the longer you stay in it, the harder it is to get out. Your mind keeps obsessing about your loss, your loneliness, and the bleakness of your future. You look at photos and cry for the days that are gone and cannot be recaptured, and the more days you spend like that, the more you believe that your situation is hopeless and that there is no future for you. I concluded that I had outlived my life and felt sentenced to continue breathing when I really did not want to do that anymore.

Thankfully, I am blessed with family members and friends who would not leave me alone and I had made some commitments that I felt a responsibility to keep. I began going through the motions of my life, without interest or joy, but I was moving and I was getting out of the house.

I had different types of connections and different ways of connecting. My son's widow needed the support that I could give her as much as I needed to support her. The only family she had nearby consisted of her daughter and me, even though neither of us was in her neighborhood; we were the closest. I don't think that I am unusual in needing to be needed. I knew that Albert would always need me, not for practical purposes, but because I was his Mom. Now, his widow was bereaved, lost and alone and she needed me. That was sufficient incentive to get me out of the house, wearing a smiley face when I could manage it, to spend time with her. We cried together and found things to laugh about and we shopped and shopped.

My grandson needed me too, and I made sure that he knew that I was there for him whenever he wanted me to be, but I did not force the issue. My granddaughter did not want to discuss her loss with me, perhaps because she thought that would cause me more pain or perhaps she was just not ready to deal with her Dad's death and I respected that. I did not push myself on either of them, but let them both know that they could count on me. I guess it comforted me more than it comforted them; but, it was important to me to be there for them.

My other grandchildren were loving and supportive, too, but I did not see much of any of them. They all had busy lives and I was glad to see them getting on with their dreams.

All of my nieces and nephews live in another state, as do my cousins, but they continue to be a great comfort to me. Most of our communication is via email, but there are occasional visits and phone calls. Email has made a huge difference in my ability to stay connected with some people. I could not afford lengthy long distance calls, nor could they, but many of us already had computers and internet access and that made email free.

One of the major forces in getting me out of the house and the ruts are my exercise buddies. I had led them to get memberships in my health club and felt obligated to get back into those routines. When I knew one of them was going to be waiting for me at the gym, I would go. Left to my own devices, I would have stayed home.

There were regular invitations to lunch, to "ride with me while I do this errand," to shop, to go to a movie, a lecture, a concert or a craft show. Someone was always doing something and asking me along. I did not always want to go, but how could I turn them down when they were so good to me; besides, when I would go, I would enjoy myself and feel better when I got home.

Then there were my neighbors with offers of support

and friendly greetings. I don't live in a small town or a neighborhood like South Philly, where everyone knows their neighbors. I live in a condominium community and only know a few of them. One of my neighbors was a good friend of Albert's and he had heard what happened. When I arrived home alone the night of Albert's death, I took off my coat, fed the cats, and sat staring at the wall until there was an urgent knock on my front door. When I opened it, I saw John, Albert's friend, with tears in his eyes. He wanted to know if I was alright and if I was alone. He seemed appalled when I told him that I was. Then he asked me if I needed anything and offered to go out and get anything I needed. I declined his offer with thanks and he sat there and talked to me for a while. I don't know how long he stayed, but it made it easier for me to get up off the couch and do what had to be done when he left.

I was touched and comforted by notes and flowers from members of groups to which I belong (e.g. DAR and the Condominium Association Board). In one case, I got a beautiful note from the Church where I grew up. Those things mean so much more than I think the people who send them can possibly understand.

All of these things and many not mentioned helped me to begin to get back into my life, to make the changes I had to make, to accept the way things are now. Those connections gave me love and, in time, helped me find hope for the future. I will never underestimate again the power of being connected to others. "People do need people."

§

Some comments about journaling. Writing was always an outlet for me and I had kept diaries and journals for most of my life. It was when Evie died that they took on more meaning and offered me a way of expressing my feelings honestly without causing others the pain of hearing how much I hurt. I have always found that writing out the pain or the problem helps me to see it from a different perspective and leads to resolutions and relief. I think better on paper, or now on keyboard.

You can tell anything to a therapist, but things that you can say to a stranger safely might hurt someone you love. Although what you say may not be about them, they may be hurt by your pain because they love you. As for therapy, the therapist is not there when you might need him/her the most. You must hold on to the issue until the appointment, but your journal is always there. This is not to suggest that a journal replaces a good therapist; not at all. However, it is there when you are alone and in addition to the other advantages of journaling, it can be a tool to take to therapy.

All About Family

The reader said, "You are all about family and it has gone wrong." It hit me as a stunning blow. I am all about family, but I no longer have one. That is what went wrong, but I can't tell if he knows.

My Albert could not find his way out of the maze that his life had become. He struggled to get back into the game, but his health problems defeated him at 41 years of age. After a successful career in construction, his body was badly damaged. He had herniated discs in his spine, he had surgery on both rotator cuffs in his shoulders and the second operation was botched and led to his death. He had, years before, had a knee replacement, he had scoliosis and arthritis and, in short, he was living in the body of a much older man. He was a big man at 6'7". When he became so disabled that moving was difficult, he put on weight, but he was always a handsome man and took care to look good. He enjoyed quality clothing and jewelry and wore them well.

The disability caused financial difficulties and he wanted the best for his wife and children. The financial problems demoralized and depressed him. He was not trained for any other type of work and was reluctant to give up his chosen field, so he struggled with therapy, with finances and with being the best father, husband and son that he could be. He was totally determined to get well and no man ever loved his family more than he did or tried harder to recover; subconsciously, I think that he was exhausted from the efforts. At one point in his illness, I told him "I can't lose you." He responded, "You won't lose me, Mom." But, I did.

Three years before he died he sent me the following in an email with a photo of him on a hunting trip.

"Mom Life is so unpredictable. Changes always come along… in big ways and small steps, sometimes giving us a little nudge and other times turning our world upside down. So many changes; some subtle and almost unnoticeable, some drastic and almost impossible to deal with. But throughout all of life's changing and rearranging. I'm so glad that there is one wonderful thing that will never change… In the passing of life's moments, I know that yesterday is already gone and that tomorrow will soon be here. The one thing that I will take with me all the days that lie ahead… is the one thing that has seen me through so many times in the past. It is something that will never change. You are such a steady, strong, and beautiful part of my life. You will never cease to amaze me with the constancy of your giving, the unselfishness of your heart, and the reassurance of your smile. And I thought it would be nice to let you know that my special feelings for you are going to last for ever and ever. AND THAT IS ONE THING THAT WILL NEVER CHANGE."

That was my son. He was loving and protective. I recall one time shortly before his death that he took me to the train in the evening. It was very cold and windy. I put my arm through his and stood as close to him as I could get. I told him that I was using him for a windbreak. He smiled and said, "Lexi does the same thing and I stand with her the same way we are standing now to keep her warm." His love for her showed in his eyes as he enjoyed that memory. On another similar occasion, there was a young man on the platform who had too much to drink and Albert went to the conductor and several of the other passengers to ask them to make sure the man did not bother me. Then, he took him aside and "explained things." When I took the train shortly after his death, the same conductor came to talk to me and ask about him. Albert was a presence. People did not forget him, even if they only met him once.

My girl has been gone for 25 years now and I have never stopped missing her or thinking how different our lives would have been if she had lived. It is doubtful that I will have to feel this new pain for another 25 years; I guess that is the good news. Or, maybe it is all good news and I can't see that for the tears and the pain of losing them.

She was afraid of her future, although she covered her fear very well with a bravado that did her credit. She need not have worried; she did not have a future on this earth in this life. After she died, my sister dreamed that she saw her walking toward her grandmothers, whose arms were outstretched. Evie's 18 years had not been easy. She was too big, too smart and too confident when she started school. They soon took the confidence out of her. When it came time for her to graduate, she did not know where she was going or how she would get there. With all of her talents (music, art, poetry), she was insecure and frightened and needed more support than she was getting.

As I wrote earlier, she died in her sleep when staying with friends, and we never found a cause. Adult SIDS death is what the coroner's office told me; later, I read about SADS (Sudden Arrhythmia Death Syndrome.)

Whatever the physical cause, I know that I am not the only person who believes that we choose when we will die, although we may not be consciously aware of making the choice. Consciously, she was working hard to get good grades to qualify for college, she was working hard at her music and performance and she was always there for her friends and family. She was full of life, love and expectations and she was not a quitter, but she had more than her share of obstacles to overcome to gain her goals. Perhaps, her soul needed to go home and rest.

My opinions are just that and, although shared by many, they are not shared by all. However, I believe that each child chooses when to be born and selects his/her parents. Each child knows what Karma needs to be worked out in a lifetime and this governs the choice of parent and time. Further, I believe that each child determines his/her exit time. S/he knows when they have accomplished all that they can in a given lifetime and when they need to depart a life. I don't think that this is a conscious decision; it is a soul decision and made at a different level than consciousness.

Their father and I divorced many years ago and I never remarried, so I am alone at 67 with no family, and I am still all about family. I lost half my heart when Evie died and the other half when Albert died. There is no heart left in me, but still something beats and I live. I have grandchildren, nieces and nephews that I do love deeply; I have two cats like babies, who are adored and spoiled, whose purr's comfort and calm me and I have daughters-in-law, a few cousins and some wonderful friends, for all of whom I am grateful and all of whom I love.

The reader goes on: He says, "Your friends are your family and your work associates are your family. You nurture others and they seek you out for nurturing. You make your own family." Do I? If I am to have one, I guess that must be done. Maybe, I do need to try and find a job. Can a 67 year old woman find a job that she is able to do and that gives some kind of satisfaction with the paycheck? A group of workers can be like a family, so can a church group; I have seen both situations work for some of my friends.

There is also my ancestral family, becoming more and more real to me as I pursue the family history. Yes, I am the family historian. Why not? I am all about family! I have documented several family lines and learned about some ancestors who did not live long enough for me to meet them, like my Grandmother Matthews. I have an ancestor wall of photographs in my front room directly above my computer, where I do the work of researching the lines.

There is comfort in that work for me. I hope that it may help to bring the family closer together (there I go again). But in addition to that benefit, the march of the generations through time is comforting. "Nobody gets out of this world alive." We all live our lives and die in God's time and plan. I am just part of that procession and will march and die when the time is right.

I find so many baby deaths in these histories and see the little stones in cemeteries. It makes me grateful for 18 years with my daughter and 41 with my son. The ancestors become living, breathing people to me as I learn about them and, again, I am comforted.

So, I guess I do have a scattered kind of family, but not the family of my heart. The assignment is to let them go, knowing their deaths were about them and not about me, and to make a new life for myself alone. It is not my choice, but God's, and He knows best. I must have more Karma to work out in this life before I can move on and I think it must be all about family.

Two Years
January 28, 2007

It was two years ago today
Life as I knew it went away.
My son was gone, my light, my joy;
That precious, special, treasured boy,
Who'd grown and changed from child to man.
His life was lived in a short span.

I'd watched each stage come and go,
As seasons pass and children grow.
The soft, warm bundle of baby scent
Changed in a year to the toddler bent
On exploring the world and taking his part
And as he did, each year he took more of my heart.

He was not the rebel teen;
He cared too much, was never mean.
His friends were many, he loved his life
And when quite young, he took a wife.
A daughter arrived and then a son;
He had never had such fun.

He loved his family most of all
And took great pride as they grew tall.
He was a big man, who was all heart,
Who gave of himself all his life from the start.
He wanted to be here for us; this I know;
But, God had decided that he had to go.

We have to believe that it's for the best;
That God knew he was tired and he needed to rest.
So, He sent the angels to bring him back home
To be with his sister; he is not alone.
Forever remembered and of my heart the king,
In spite of the sting that the memories bring.

Ready for Santa's delivery

Evie in 2nd grade, Albert in kindergarten

Looking Back

January 2007

For a while after Albert died, I was obsessed with trying to see into the future. The future I had expected was history now and all that I could see was that the dark cloud that had visited me in the past was now completely obliterating my future. I simply could not see ahead.

When we can't see where to step, most of us would take small, careful steps and try to find landmarks, I think. As I look back on that time, that is what I did. Not that I knew what I was doing at the time; my goal was just getting through each day and trying to find some comfort as I went along.

I tried to remember who I was before I married, before I was a mother or a grandmother. Who was Mignon and what did she want from life (excepting what she had lost)? The song that haunted me after Evie died came back into my head. It was just one line from MacArthur Park and it was about the loss of something very precious that had taken a long time to create and that could never be duplicated.

Evie was a rebellious teen and we had some tough times during her early teenage years, mostly about her choice of friends and her frustration with our rules. She did not want any restrictions or any advice and she wanted to behave like a fully grown and independent adult, which she was not. This is not a unique situation between parents and teenagers and from what I see on TV, it is even more prevalent today.

One night, we ran out of milk and so I was going out to get some for breakfast. I asked her if she wanted to go with me and she did, which was good news in itself. We listened to the car radio, talked a little, laughed a little and merely enjoyed being together. When we pulled into the driveway at home, that song was playing on the radio. I admitted to Evie that this song haunted me when she was "acting out" and that I was so grateful to be past that period and see her on the right track again. She responded, "Mom, don't count on it. Just don't count on it." She did not say it in a belligerent manner or as a joke. She was completely serious and gentle about it. I think that she wanted me to know that she was not sure how things would work out and she wanted me to be prepared if I was disappointed. She would not explain further, but the shadow came over my heart again that night.

I'll return now to the point I was attempting to make, which is that the song I referred to above had become my theme song again. I really did not know if I could make it this time and I was searching for the core of me, the part that was there from my beginning; it seemed to me that was all that I had left. You see, that core had so many layers wrapped over it through the years from the life I had lived that I was not sure I could find it anymore.

I believed that God had a plan for me, but could not imagine what it might be. Why would I be here without either of my children? What was the point? I could not see anything ahead, so I looked back. I was asking myself what I wanted to be and liked to do way back then, and would I still like to do or be now.

The first thing that I always knew I wanted to be was a wife and mother. I always played with dolls, paper dolls, doll dishes, etc. I knew that I had to have that and I got it. For a time, my marriage was quite happy and our children were wonderful. But that is over and I can't have that ever again. Perhaps, I could find a companion, but I am getting a bit "long in the tooth and set in my ways" for that to be likely. I am blessed with wonderful grandchildren, two of Albert's own and three of his stepchildren. They are all the grandchildren of my heart, but they are grown and busy with their lives, so contact with them is lovely but rare.

The second thing that I always loved to do was sing and I had that too. I sang professionally from a very early age and I got a degree in music education. But, physical problems developed in my late 40's, probably age related, and limited the singing I can do even in a church choir. I still play the piano occasionally, although I have never been very good at it and I realized, as I considered this, that I have one thing going in that regard; I accompany a group of women and am the official musician for the local chapter of the LGAR (Ladies of the Grand Army of the Republic.) It is a patriotic organization, which I joined shortly after retiring and which I do enjoy. They only require my services as musician once a year, but I look forward to that responsibility.

That awareness caused the fog to clear a bit. Now I thought about the other groups I had joined after retirement; the DAR and the Colonial Dames of the XVII Century and I remembered how that had come about. I had always had an interest in the family history, but never had time to really get into it until I retired. My retirement gift to myself was a new computer and then I discovered the joys of online research. I had soon enough found lots of ancestors who came to the New World early on and documenting them qualified me for membership in those organizations. I met some very nice and like-minded women through these meetings and my research, and they have added a new dimension to my life. Of course, I got involved by accepting positions and that enabled me to get to know people better as well as have a feeling of accomplishment for the good that the groups do for veterans, Indian schools and other charities.

Those things had led to my volunteering as a Docent at a Revolutionary Tavern Museum and to becoming involved with a group formed to raise funds for the restoration of the tavern. Oh yes, now I recall that I was always interested in history and I have been acting that out without being aware of the "core" interest.

I started writing down the things that I am currently doing with the groups to which I belong and realized that I had missed the group that takes more of my time than any of the others. I have served on the Board of Trustees for my condominium association for many years, most of them as president, and I have derived much satisfaction from the work we have accomplished for our community.

This group feels much more like a job than the others, but in spite of the difficulties that are certain to surface in this type of activity, there is the gratification of knowing that I am making a positive difference in my community. This was never something that I dreamed of doing, not one of my "core" interests, but it was related to one that I discovered when I entered the world of business and that is that I like solving problems and organizing things.

That lead to a new train of thought and an examination of the interests that I discovered as an adult; they can be "core" interests too. I recalled that I enjoyed teaching/training. I have worked as a substitute teacher, a teacher's aide, a piano and voice instructor and a software trainer for insurance companies.

And, I loved the written word. I always wrote for my own pleasure; stories or poems. I did some technical writing for the insurance industry, and many, many business letters and reports.

To sum it up, I was gradually able to remember things that I liked to do when I was more in touch with my inner spirit and I still liked to do some of them, if not all. In fact, I was already involved in some of these things and when I went for emotional support and guidance, my therapist advised that I journal; that was the beginning of this book.

Over the years, I have come to believe that the things that you feel compelled to do are the things God wants you to do. Otherwise, why would you want to do them? We are all given potential at our arrival on this planet. The thing is to discover our talents and interests and use them to our advantage and the advantage of others. The things we do don't have to be big, important things, but our job is to do what we can with what is ours.

I won't say that any of this was easy or happened quickly, but I learned when I lost my Evie that I had a decision to make. I could live or I could die. Because I still had my Albert, the decision was made for me; I would never willingly abandon him and I did not. Now, the decision was mine alone to make. When I lost him, the only living beings that needed me were my cats, and I knew who would take good care of them if I died. So, this time I decided to live the rest of my life as fully as possible – for me. Life still hurts. A memory sneaks up on me and brings me to my knees on a regular basis, but I cry it out, I write it out and I get on with it. There are many good days.

My faith helps, because I know that I will be with both of them again and I fill up with joy when I contemplate what that will be like. But today, I enjoyed the sun streaming through the windows, the warmth of the house after going outside into the cold of February, the soft furry, purry affection of my cats and the blessing of having everything I need to be comfortable and things to do that I enjoy. I have much for which to be grateful and I take the time to give thanks.

Albert with baby Lexi (above); with Alby's cake (below)

Two Plus Twenty Five

My Evie girl, my golden child,
So very sweet, a little wild.
So full of life and plans and joy
A little bold, a little coy.

The child I always dreamed as mine,
The one I asked from God Devine.
The prayer was granted and she came
On New Year's Eve, which suits her name.

A little brother followed soon
And we were all "over the moon."
She loved her "Bro" and gave him toys;
Ignored him when he made loud noise.

She played guitar and wrote some songs,
She sang and danced and all along
She loved and laughed and tossed her curls.
She was her Mommy's precious girl.

God took her home, it seemed too soon.
The light had gone out of the moon,
The sun was dark and life was grey,
Because my darling went away.

The date came round in all the years,
Twenty-seven without her, celebrated with tears.
So much to remember of those yesterdays,
So much to recall of her matchless ways.

I guess she is now strumming her guitar
In the Angels band that's away so far
From us, but close to God and now
To Bro as well, her favorite pal.

I know my angels are in God's place;
Together forever in Heaven's space,
And one day, if I qualify
I'll be with them, no more to cry.

Alby and Lexi watching a Christmas show

Grandchildren

I never could get enough of them; I enjoyed them so much. Unfortunately, having to earn my living and location got in the way of my "grand-mothering." Albert and I both lived in the Philadelphia area of New Jersey, but at some distance from each other and I worked in Philadelphia. This made it difficult to impossible for me to pick up one of them after school or to take care of them on short notice.

So, I did what I could do and had them for "overnights" as often as possible. I liked to get them one at a time, so that we had one on one interactions and I could just focus my spoiling on the grandchild at hand.

1989 was the first of the Christmas jaunts for Billy and me and the first time for Lexi and me too; each was a separate trip. That was the year that Alby was born, so he had to stay home. Each child would come for an overnight and we would go into the city for the day. I would let him or her pick out one Christmas present when we shopped and we visited all of the Christmas attractions: Colonial Village, the Wanamaker's Light Show and Dickens Village. Sometimes, we took carriage rides and we always went into the city on the commuter train, which was also a treat for them.

On our first Christmas excursion, Lexi was fascinated by the escalators, so we had to change floors a lot. She was totally terrified of the Dicken's exhibit, so we did not see much of that the first time. Billy, on the other hand, loved the Dickens exhibit, and especially the light show and carriage rides. When I would snap a picture of him, he would want to snap one of me and we loved to walk down Market Street singing the Twelve Days of Christmas at the "top of our lungs."

From his first trip, Alby loved all of it! I remember one year, he wanted to have lunch in the Wanamaker lunchroom, so we did. This was not our usual dining choice, as they all usually preferred pizza, but something about the dining room intrigued Alby. There were cloth tablecloths and napkins and he loved every minute of it until he got his dessert; not that he didn't love it, but he ordered a sundae that overfilled the glass dish and he was very worried about getting ice cream on the tablecloth. He was the perfect little gentleman and I was so proud of him. The waitresses could not do enough for him in spite of the busy lunch hour.

Of course, a highlight was the visit to the Santa at Strawbridge and Clothier. That was the BEST one and I have lots of pictures to prove it. One of my favorites was not taken at S&C, however, but in the Gallery Mall. Lexi spotted Santa and although she had already visited the S&C Santa, she wanted to talk to this one too; just to be on the safe side with her list. He was a very friendly fellow and asked me if I did not want to sit on his knee too; so we each got a knee and I have a priceless photo of that day.

There is only one thing wrong with grandchildren; they grow up too soon and they get very busy. As I write this, Billy has graduated from college and is starting his first "real" job. Lexi is now in her sophomore year of college and Alby is a senior in high school and headed for college in the fall.

So far, I have only talked about my first three grandchildren, but with Albert's third marriage, I got two more; David and Kelly. Of course, we did not do Santa visits, as Kelly had just graduated high school and David was finishing up when I got them. They did not want to go do the Christmas ritual with me in Philadelphia. What was up with that? No matter, I had seen it all quite a few times.

Kelly is now happily married and expecting my first great-grandson. I was honored to read at her wedding and have learned to love Kelly, David and Kevin, Kelly's husband. David is career Air Force and has just finished his second tour in Kuwait. We are SO glad to have him home. He is my hero.

So, I am blessed with grandchildren and deeply grateful that they are the fine young people that they have become. I miss those children and their lives are too full and too busy for me to see much of them now, but I know they are out there making their individual marks in the world and that makes me happy and proud.

It is good to be a grandparent!

I wrote the following poem, *Umbrellas*, not too long after Lexi started grade school.

Umbrellas

Was my first umbrella a black watch plaid?
No, bright red and green was the first one I had.
I flaunted its beauty with youthful pride,
As I waited for the bus to ride.

My girl's first umbrella was yellow and blue;
A bright plastic bubble kept her dry as she grew.
As right for the 60's as plaid was for me,
We each prized our symbol of conformity.

Does my little granddaughter have one of her own?
I love her so dearly, but I haven't known
Much about her treasures and secrets and pain,
And now she's a schoolgirl with her own domain.

But probably that is just as it should be,
Her parents know all that about their baby,
And Grandmom must recognize that and let go.
It's time for the next act, so on with the show.

We can love each other in a most special way;
Go places together and share lots of play;
Be confidants, buddies, share laughter and tears
When we both find the time in the vanishing years.

All About My Health

In my journals, I have spilled out my emotions; my fears, resentments, sorrows and my joys. I have delved into spiritual matters too, asking myself questions, making assumptions, testing some theories and finding myself sometimes right, sometimes wrong and sometimes clueless. The only attention that I have given to my physical body in my journals consists of weight loss/gain charts and lists of diet plans. Weight has been an obsession for me for most of my life, often out of control, and there is a reason for that too.

Grief is a physical thing as much as an emotional thing; it affects our bodies. I am not a medical expert; I am just someone who reads a lot and reduces what she finds to overall concepts and personal experience, and I have come to believe strongly in the mind/body connection. I know that there are substances released in our bodies when we are under stress that can do us harm. Losing a child is the worst stress that can happen to a parent and it is a time for taking the best care of ourselves, of reducing other stresses to the extent possible and of letting go of unimportant things to concentrate on healing and finding peace and joy again.

For example, I start with my weight problem. When my life is going well and I am at least reasonably happy, my weight goes down and my mood goes up accordingly. When I am sick, unhappy or grieving, my weight knows only one direction to go and I am now twenty pounds heavier than I was on the day my son died a little over two years ago. Food comforts and calms me, so I eat it. Wine relaxes me and helps me fall asleep, so I drink it. Since I lost Albert, my bedtime snack has gone to new levels of calories and my body to new levels of weight. I read and hear from experts that the secret is to replace one bad habit with one good habit, but when you are grieving, how much do you care? When will I reach a place where I do care for more than three weeks at a time? I hope it will be before I reach 200 pounds; I am only 5'4" tall with a small frame. There have been a few weeks that occurred two or three times in this period when I got it under control and lost some weight, but then another issue would come up and my need for the comfort offered by food and wine outweighed (pardon the pun) my desire to take better care of myself. It is an uphill battle for me, but I will not give up the fight. I work hard at recovering from my losses and I will continue to persevere; I will not give up and I will reach my goals in time.

One of the most helpful things I have done is to walk. Walking calms and energizes me and it helps to control my weight. I had worked my way up to fifty minutes five or six days a week; I was losing weight and feeling much better. I was sleeping well, because exercise does that for me too and I had two walking partners; one for a.m. walking and one for p.m. walking. When I was employed, I would often walk at lunch time and then again after work. It is more fun with a partner, but a portable CD player will also be good company and it is inexpensive; of course, an iPOD or MP3 Player would be lighter and better, but more expensive. The point is that music helps you keep your pace up and will also lighten your mood if you choose the right music. It should be upbeat music with a good steady beat, but it must be music that you enjoy. I have enjoyed walking to classical music and also New Age. Some of it was not what you would term "good walking music," but I like it, it lifted my mood and it helped me think positive thoughts while I walked.   Walking can be a meditation, which leads me to something else that helps me.

Many people still believe that mediation is "woo woo" stuff; that one must chant a mantra in a yogic position and stare at a candle. Not so. All that you need to do to meditate is to breathe deeply and empty your mind OR focus on a specific topic or thing. If you are walking at a good pace, breathing deeply comes naturally and if you are walking in nature, meditation comes easily; at least it does for me. I also meditate at home and in church, among other places. It calms me and I find answers to problems come "out of the blue" during meditation. The thing is (in my opinionated opinion) that prayer and meditation go hand in hand. I am Protestant and meditation has not been a part of my early experience in the church, but I have found that some Protestant churches do practice it now. When we pray, we ask God for direction; when we meditate, we listen for his answer. That is the still small voice you hear in your heart that helps you solve your problems. There are many good books on meditation in any book store. It is really very simple, but I like to read on every subject that interests me, so I would suggest reading about it too.

Another option would be a meditation class and they are often offered at community colleges and sometimes at adult evening schools.

Sometimes, obstacles come into your path despite your best intentions and that just happened to me. I hurt one of my knees and developed a Bakers Cyst, resulting in instructions from my rheumatologist to reduce my walking to routine tasks for a time to let it heal. You can imagine how I felt about that, but I followed orders and it is well on the way to being healed. In fact, I got permission to use the stationary bikes at the health club and they help too. I like to get there three times a week and I do weights and the bike.

When you are grieving, it is very important to get out with other people and you may not always want to go. Especially in winter, I want to hibernate when I am sad, but I have partners at the health club who will nag me into going and I am almost always glad when I get there. The lights, the sounds, the activity; they all combine to bring me back into life. A mall can do some of the same things. Humans are social animals and we need each other whether we like it or not.

Since my retirement, I have fallen into the habit of napping in the afternoon; not every afternoon, but when I get the urge and I feel better for it. After I lost Albert, I napped just about every day and slept through every night, but that was a good thing. You heal when you sleep, your body relaxes completely and it heals best when at rest. Those harmful substances that are shooting through our bodies under grief are stopped cold when we completely relax and that is another reason to meditate as well. In fact, many people fall asleep while meditating. Now that I think of it, meditation accounts for many of my naps.

There is one more thing that is vital to our recovery and I don't use that word lightly. Losing a child is like an illness that has no magic pill and we need to work at recovery. The one more thing is nutrition. The lethargy that often accompanies grief encourages a dinner that consists of a bagel with cream cheese and a dish of ice cream. Not a good idea. In taking care of ourselves, we can make it easy to eat well with just a little planning. Fresh vegetables and fruit require little to no effort on our part. A salad and a low fat frozen dinner is not such a bad thing and how hard is it to open a can of soup and toast a piece of wheat bread to go with it? When I don't feel like cooking (which is most of the time), I will do things like that or make a grilled cheese sandwich on my kitchen grill. That is great with a cup of tomato soup. And a crock pot is a wonderful thing for easy meals. Just put some fresh carrots and sliced onions in the bottom add a pot roast and seasonings and let it cook itself.

A little care with meals makes you feel better physically and that helps you recover emotionally.

I also take vitamin supplements in case I am not getting good nutrition from my diet. As we age, I think that our bodies may not always utilize the nutrients we get from food; so, I take an extra precaution. During good times and bad I have taken the supplements and they have definitely helped me to stay healthy.

How else have I managed to survive so far? I read

for escape as well as for knowledge and inspiration. I don't always get out to church, but I do watch the Hour of Power every week and have for years. Dr. Schuller is the voice of positive Christianity and his talks are always motivating and leave me feeling hopeful, even if I cry during almost every service.

My choices won't suit everybody, but maybe my experience will suggest some things that will work for others and that is my hope in sharing my own efforts with you. I don't have all the answers, but after losing so many people and struggling to overcome my pain and sadness, I have learned some things that work for me. Clearly, I still have things to work out and I will continue to read, pray, meditate and try new methods. That has worked for me and I need to keep on keeping on.

Two Forward, One Back
February 2007

As I review this, I keep asking myself the same questions. Is it too whiney? Is it depressing? Will anybody relate to it? Does the part about my early life matter or does it just fill pages? Could my experience help anybody or will the readers, if there are any, simply wonder at the waste of time, consider it a pity party and toss it into the trash? After the passing of another year, I still don't know; I have let my thoughts float from my mind to the paper, much as they came to me and that is what I want to share.

Whatever happens, writing it helped me through a terrible time in my life and now I can see that I do have a life. I was a person in my own right before I married and had children and I am still that person. So, I do what seems right for me to do one day at a time, relying on prayer and meditation for guidance and direction. There are things I want to do and, in my opinion, those are the things God wants me to do; otherwise, why would I want them?

This small book was one of those things, so I will try to get it published in the hope that it will help others who are grieving to read my little story. In the last year, life has gone on and I have begun re-entry. Some things I have done/am doing follow.

I have re-established regular communication with my

grandchildren by taking all responsibility for it on myself; after all, I am the grandmother and what I want to offer them is unconditional love and acceptance with no strings attached. They have lost so much, and I want to be there for them if and when they want to be with me.

My daughter-in-law's possible departure to far away places no longer holds the apprehension that it initially did for me. Although I would prefer to have her near me, I believe that the bond between us will not vanish with her move.

My nieces, nephews, and cousins play a larger role in my life than before the loss of my son, and their loving support has helped me so much more than I know how to tell them. I take care to keep in close contact with them and will continue to do whatever I can to nourish those relationships.

Friends greatly bless my life every day and have been with me and there for me constantly throughout this ordeal. Sadly, I have discovered that some friends cannot handle my loss and there are two dearly loved women with whom I am no longer in contact. It is my conclusion, knowing them both very well, that my pain hurts them and the reality that the same thing could happen to them terrifies them. I bless them on their way with gratitude for what we have been to and for each other. There are some other friends who are not comfortable with me, because they too feel my pain, but they are sticking it out and sticking with me. These relationships are getting a little easier and can be expected to fall back to the way we were in time. This, I firmly believe.

The un-cluttering of my life goes forward at a slow pace, but it does progress. As I give away things I no longer use or want, it gives me a sense of relief to be rid of them that is nearly equal to the satisfaction of giving to someone who will enjoy and appreciate them as I did in the past.

When I un-clutter, I make space for something or new things, or I enjoy the space. It is too soon to know which will happen, but whatever it is, I am confident it will be for my highest good. That is why it is so important. It has finally become apparent to me that holding on to things does not keep the people associated with those things in my life. So obvious, but it was a difficult lesson for me to learn. There are things I will never part with for the sweet memories they evoke, like the fleece shirt that my son wrapped me in when I was cold at his house or the little handprint in clay that my daughter brought home from kindergarten, but I am evaluating the things I have kept for sentimental reasons and making choices.

My long term interest in my family history has been a source of much enjoyment and of meeting some wonderful people. It has led to joining the LGAR (Ladies of the Grand Army of the Republic), the DAR (Daughters of the American Revolution) and the Colonial Dames of the 17th Century. Becoming involved in these groups with whom I have much in common, and making new friends in the groups and on-line during research, has enriched my days and my life. It has also brought me closer to some members of my family and it is to be hoped that it is bringing them closer to each other.

It just occurred to me one day while I was sitting in the swing on my back deck that I was a person before I married and had those precious children and I am still that person. Throughout my life, I have been interested in history and in our family history; now I have time to explore it and there are so many places I want to visit that are related to that interest.

That brings me to another subject: finances. I am "under funded" for a long life, giving me a choice of dying before I run out of money or getting more money. Do I look for a job? The obvious answer is "yes." My health is good, overall, and what I could earn from a part time job would help with the travel kitty in addition to helping with day-to-day expenses. A full-time job would be more lucrative, of course, but I do not feel up to that, given the toll that the years and events of those years have taken on my energy. That said, there would not be enough time for travel if I worked full-time anyway. So part-time employment is the way I want to go and not just for the paycheck.

It is also a way of starting over, of meeting new people, learning new skills and getting out in the world. I think it will be quite a challenge and require some creativity on my part to find a part time job at my age, but challenges are good for the brain and spirit.

When I think about how busy I keep myself without holding down a job, I wonder how I am going to manage it. There are the routine tasks that must be done, like paying the bills, cleaning the house, getting the car serviced, doing the laundry, shopping and keeping up my health. That in itself takes some time at my age.

- There is nutrition; and, I need to plan, shop for, and cook healthy meals.
- I need to devise and follow a weight loss plan.
- There is exercise; I need to continue to work out with weights, walk and bike to stay in shape and help to control my weight.
- There must be time for reflection, prayer and meditation.
- There must be time for worship, study, and growth.
- There must be time for fun with friends and family.
- There must be time for social gatherings and community involvement.
- There must be time for hobbies.
- There must be time for vacations.

Finding the time and energy to balance my life will not be easy and I must prioritize and use both well. "Work smart" is the phrase I recall from my business experience. Now, I need to apply that principal to my retirement experience.

So, the first step was revamping the resume to point to a much less demanding position on a part-time basis. Step two was "doing" the want-ads, but that has not worked out too well. I only found one position of interest to me and it takes so much time to do the search, even on-line. I have decided to go a different route and start checking places that I would like to work; perhaps I might volunteer at a library to check it out and let them check me out. Also, I am looking at locations where I would enjoy working and planning to walk my resume into some of them for an opportunity to "sell" myself.

When I decided to try that one, I decided to do a little upgrade on the presentation, so I got a new hairstyle and did a review of the wardrobe. Next stop: the mall.

It was hard for me to consider looking for a job, given that I no longer have a career, and it took some reminding myself that I have a lot to offer in my experience, work ethic and abilities. When I reached that point, I began to get excited about the prospect and I am a mixture of anxious and excited now.

It is time to take the next step, but this self-assigned task needs to be completed first. I don't know if this is a good book or a bad book, if it may offer some comfort and hope or if it is depressing or maudlin; most of all, I don't know if anybody will want to print it or buy it. Nonetheless, I will finish it and my next challenge will be to get it accepted by a publisher. I hope that happens; but if it does not, I have had the satisfaction of putting my experience onto these pages and I have tried to the best of my ability to share my experience. It was what I needed to do.

Denouement

Albert's daughter graduated high school the same year that he died. We knew she was missing him that day and how much that must hurt, but she never let it show. I know he was looking down on her with such pride. All of us were still in the early stages of grief, but her graduation was a bright spot in a dark time.

In June 2007, Albert's son graduated from the same high school that Albert had attended. The last graduation ceremony that I attended there was Evie's, and she was not there to receive her diploma or toss her hat into the air with her class. Albert was by my side to attend the memorial to her and another classmate who did not make it to graduation. It was a very sad occasion for us, but we wanted to be there for her.

Seeing Albert's son graduate on that field somehow closed a circle for me. He looks so much like his dad, but with his Aunt Evie's complexion and bright blond hair. He was one of the last to receive his diploma and all of the first students to march up to the dais had sedately marched back to their seats. Not our boy. He jumped off the platform and danced to his seat with his arms in the air.

His mother told me that he chose to wear his dad's watch and we all knew that he was thinking about him. It seemed that he wanted the world to know that he was proud of what he had done and that he was moving forward in his life with joy. That is exactly what his dad would want for him.

It is likely that Albert's children will marry and have children of their own. Sadly, those children will never know their grandfather, so they will never know what they missed by his absence; however, Albert left his mark on his children and they will know how to give the love, support, comfort, and guidance that he gave to them. They will be wonderful parents. That will be part of his legacy to them and it will be the best way they can ever honor his memory.

Write-on
by EvieG - 1979

Sometimes,
It's easier to write
Than to speak directly.

In a poem,
I cannot be rejected,
Only praised or criticized for my form.

In a poem,
I can show my feelings toward you
Without requiring that yours be revealed.

A poem gives you time;
It gives you the freedom of choosing
Whether to let your emotions be known.
Or not to.

Silently, in time,
Your feelings become known to me.
You are already aware of mine;
Feelings too strong to say.

So, on I write.

Did you like *Mom No More?*

Do you need more copies for friends and relatives? Of course you do! Order directly from the publisher at www.geroproducts.com, through your local bookstore, or use the order form below (may be photocopied).

Also, you may be interested in our other books and gifts:

Qty __ *Mom No More: Coping With the Late-Life Loss of Adult Children - One Woman's Story* by Mignon Matthews - $29.95

A widow is a woman whose husband has died and an orphan is a child whos parents are both dead, but what is a woman whose children are dead? There is no name for them, but they exist. The author lost both of her children after they were adults - her daughter Evie at 18 and her son Albert at 42. This is her story of coping with the depression, pain, anger, and injustice of outliving her beloved children.

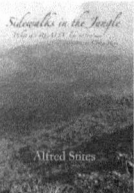

Qty __ *Sidewalks in the Jungle: What it's REALLY Like to Retire and Live in Costa Rica* by Alfred Stites - $35.95

This book deals with the reality of moving to, and living in htis beautiful and stable Central American democracy. Topics covered span from managing maids and gardeners to trips to the doctor and avoiding violent street crime.

The Healthy Seniors Cookbook: Ideal Meals and Menus for People Over Sixty (Or Any Age) by Marilyn McFarlane - $19.95

Whether cooking for yourself, your spouse, or visiting grandchildren, this book features an easy-to-read, easy-to-use format that provides flavorful meals and simple, fast cooking methods.

Seniors in Love: A Second Chance for Single, Divorced and Widowed Seniors by Robert Wolley - $19.95

This well-reviewed book deals with the emotional, financial, physical, and other relevant issues facing seniors when considering a new, intimate relationship.

The Greatest Companion: Reflections on Life, Love and Marriage After 60 by Robert Wolley - $19.95

Through prose and poetry, this book explores the joys of late-in-life love, provides reminders of what such a love needs to flourish, and reflects upon love's agelessness.

ABC's for Seniors: Successful Aging Wisdom from an Outrageous Gerontologist by Ruth Jacobs - $19.95

In this book, Dr. Jacobs presents the essentials that enable a reader to harvest life fully for creative, healthy, successful, vigorous, and meaningful aging.

Qty — *Seniors in Love* car magnet - $11.95
Show the world that love knows no age! An ideal wedding or anniversary gift! Measures six by four inches, in red, white, and gold. Removable. Fits any RV!

Qty — *"Grow old along with me"* mug - $9.95
Robert Browning said it, but it's as true today as it was 100 years ago! Illustration and quote, printed in black on both sides. Truly, *"the best is yet to be"*

Name   _____

Address   _____

City/State/Zip   _____

Please mark the products you want, and their quantity (Missouri residents only please add 5.25% sales tax).

There is no charge for shipping and handling, and all orders are shipped from Greentop, Missouri (population 427).

Send check or money order to:
Hatala Geroproducts
PO Box 42
Greentop, MO 63546

What makes Hatala Geroproducts different?

Hatala Geroproducts of Greentop, Missouri, was founded in 2002. An independent company, Hatala Geroproducts publishes books, games, magnetic signs, and greeting cards primarily for seniors. The focus is on relationships: with spouses, lovers, other seniors, grandchildren, and adult children.

• All products are "age positive," which means that they are respectful to seniors, and focus on the positive aspects of aging.

• All books are "larger print" for easier reading.

• Books are written by senior authors for senior readers.

• All products are developed with the help of academic gerontologists and seniors themselves.

• Hatala Geroproducts is dedicated to remain an earth-friendly, sustainable, carbon-neutral company.

We thank you for your continued support!

If you have any questions or comments, feel free to contact me personally at mark@geroproducts.com

Mark Hatala, Ph.D.
President, Hatala Geroproducts
Professor of Psychology, Truman State University

Notes

Notes